M000033142

SELLING
WITH POWER

SELLING
WITH POWER

The Base, Blocks and Blueprint to
build a sales career powered by God

JOHN J. KIMMEL

AUTHOR
ACADEMY elite

LINDA
I PRAY THIS BOOK IS
A BLESSING!

Cover Design by Deja Vvu
Illustrations by Allison Kimmel

Copyright © 2016 John J. Kimmel
All rights reserved.

Printed in the United States of America

Published by Author Academy Elite
P.O. Box 43, Powell, OH 43035

www.AuthorAcademyElite.com

All rights reserved. No part of this publication may be reproduced,
stored in a retrieval system, or transmitted in any form or by any
means—for example, electronic, photocopy, recording—without
the prior written permission of the publisher. The only exception
is brief quotations in printed reviews.

Paperback ISBN-13: 978-1-943526-95-6

Hardcover ISBN-13: 978-1-943526-94-9

Library of Congress Control Number: 2016915620

This book is dedicated to Jesus Christ,
who called me to a purpose far higher than
I ever deserved, and to my wife Dena,
who introduced me to Him.

CONTENTS

BLUEPRINT:
THE PLAN THAT TIES IT ALL TOGETHER

FOREWORD

AVERAGE SALESPEOPLE ASK, "How can I reach my sales goals?" Elite salespeople ask, "How can I sell more than everyone else, combined?"

Throughout his career as a successful sales leader, John Kimmel was intentional about desegregating his career from his walk with God. His passion for his vocation, combined with his thirst for the Word, led him to pursue the knowledge of what God wanted from him, both at work and at home. Realizing that there didn't seem to be a single book on the topic of selling from a Christian perspective, John set out to write the book he believes will enable believers to not only dedicate their careers to their Creator, but also sell at levels far above their peers.

John started his own quest for sales knowledge while he was still a teenager. Selling carpet for his father's company, he would constantly listen to sales training tapes in his car. Filling his mind with the skills he learned from great sales trainers like Zig Ziglar and Bryan Tracy, John soon found that at a very young age, he could outperform the most seasoned veterans.

After coming to know the Lord in his early twenties, John's newly found faith led him to learn about God's heart for his work. The combination of John's faith and skill propelled him to even higher levels as he sold not just out of his own strength, but rather from a place of power in God. John now has a heart to share that power with the world.

In *Selling with Power* speaker, and sales trainer John J. Kimmel shows you "why" serving as an effective salesperson is a biblical mandate. He'll also unpack "how" this is possible no matter the circumstances. You'll discover:

- Confidence that God has called His followers to be sales people.
- The truth of what selling really is.
- The skills that are most important to create maximum sales growth.
- How to dramatically increase your close rate.
- How to bless your customer, your employer, yourself, and God at the same time.

Blending a mix of stories, research and personal experience, John shares proven principles that took him over 30 years of selling, studying, and walking with Christ to discover. These truths will power up your selling to levels you never dreamed possible.

Isn't it time you started selling with power—that place where preparation meets the will of God?

Kary Oberbrunner
Author of *ELIXIR Project*,
Day Job to Dream Job, *The Deeper Path*, and *Your Secret Name*

BASE

THE FOUNDATION OF SELLING WITH POWER

CHAPTER 1
DOES GOD REALLY
WANT YOU TO BE A
SALES PERSON?

A DAY OF SALES TRAINING

BILL STRUGGLED WITH closing sales. Recently, we chatted about his resistance. As part of our training, while discussing a particular technique, I demonstrated to him what the technique would look like and then he mirrored what I said. Ironically, Bill couldn't do it. I'd say one thing and then when it was his turn, he changed the words, his tone of voice and even his body language.

Now let me be clear, Bill is a bright young man. He didn't have any difficulty understanding or remembering what I had said. In fact, we had performed this same exercise with other parts of the sales process. He nailed them. I repeated the process, but each time, he replied in a way completely different than what the exercise required. Finally, I stopped and asked him why he struggled with the exercise.

His head dropped a bit, his eyes lowered to the floor, and with clear uneasiness in his voice he said, "I just don't want to come on so strong."

"Strong?" I asked.

"Well, you know, kind of like a used car salesman." I considered for a moment and asked, "What part of this exercise makes you feel like a used car salesman?" He continued to fidget and squirm in his chair until he finally said "It's this whole closing thing, it just makes me uncomfortable."

Bill's problem was simple. He didn't think it was possible to "sell" somebody something and be ethical at the same time.

Over the years, I have encountered this error frequently. It seems as if many believe being a great salesperson is in conflict with being a Godly person. I've talked to many believers that admit feeling uncomfortable with success. Sometimes, it even seems like they're more comfortable with struggle than success.

This phenomenon led me to write this book. I have a passion to help people become powerful salespeople. I don't mean just a little better than the crowd. I mean the kind of salespeople that outsell their peers by 200%, 500% or more. I mean the kind of salespeople that stand out from the crowd and get job offers from all their competitor's companies because everyone knows their name. I also have a passion for helping Christians understand what God really wants from their lives, including how they handle themselves at work.

Throughout this book, I will be citing scripture as the foundation for what I believe and why these principles are righteous. My goal is for you to finish this book empowered to use your sales career as a way to change your own life as well as the lives of your family. You will soon have the foundation not just for a job, but strong enough to build a career on. You will have the skills necessary to continually soar past your competition and the blueprint that brings all of these pieces together. Most importantly, I will show you why selling is an honorable, righteous profession in the eyes of our Lord and that you can follow His will and break records at the same time.

A NOBLE WIFE

One of my favorite passages of scripture comes from Proverbs. In chapter 31, Solomon describes a "Wife of noble character." I have always found it interesting that among the noble attributes he lists are, "She makes linen garments and sells them," and, "She sees that her trading is profitable."

Solomon goes on to say, "She speaks with wisdom, and faithful instruction is on her tongue" before he closes with "Honor her for all that her hands have done, and let her works bring her praise at the city gate."

There are four important "Noble" character traits we need to consider in this scripture.

1. The wife Solomon is describing *sells* things. It is important to look at scripture in the context under which it was written. In this culture, if you were making fine garments, they would have had considerable value. She also would have been selling them to experienced merchants, such as Phoenician traders, who were known for their negotiating skills. The suggestion is that she was an experienced salesperson, not just someone having a garage sale.

2. She makes a profit. Some would have you think that making a profit is somehow unethical, but the Bible says differently. While the Bible issues strong warnings to those who would profit unjustly, it makes clear that working in the right way should yield the reward of a profit.

3. She speaks with wisdom and truth. As salespeople, this is our calling. We are called to help others make the best possible decisions for themselves, their families and their companies. You have likely heard people say that a great salesperson becomes an "assistant buyer." In many ways that is true, as we will explore later.

4. All these things bring her honor. The phrase "honor her" here can also be translated as "give to her what she deserves." God rewards the righteous with riches far beyond what we can possibly imagine. Sometimes those riches are tangible, and temporal, but more often, they are eternal and priceless. Either way, when we act according to God's Word, there is a reward.

All of us are faced with choices with regard to how we conduct business. Solomon described character above not just by telling us what the noble wife believed, but more importantly, he described what she *did*. The same is true for us. Our customers do not measure our character based on what we believe, they measure our character based on what we do. More importantly, God looks at us the same way. While our salvation is not the result of what we do, what we do *will* be an outward manifestation of what we believe.

Paul is truly one of my "Salesperson" heroes. Over and over in the New Testament, you will see a word appear, and that word is persuasion. In his second letter to the

Corinthians Paul says, "Since, then, we know what it is to fear the Lord, we try to persuade others." In the book of Romans he says, "Yet he did not waver through unbelief regarding the promise of God, but was strengthened in his faith and gave glory to God, [21] being fully persuaded that God had power to do what he had promised." Again in the book of Acts Paul says, "He witnessed to them from morning till evening, explaining about the kingdom of God, and from the Law of Moses and from the Prophets he tried to persuade them about Jesus." The word persuade can mean to urge, entice, move, or compel.

These verses have one thing in common. The Apostle Paul is urging, moving, enticing and compelling these people toward something good—in this case, salvation. Paul has absolute confidence that the path he is leading these people down is truly the best thing for them. While it is good for Paul as well, ultimately, Paul is driven to persuade others because it is what's best for them.

Zig Ziglar, one of the best sales trainers that ever lived, used to say "You can get anything you want out of life, if you will just help enough other people get what they want." Zig was absolutely right. It is critical that you understand this concept if you are going to have a successful sales career and a right relationship with your Father in Heaven.

Remember Bill? The one who was having trouble closing? Bill didn't have a problem with persuasion; he just didn't understand the difference between persuasion and manipulation. Manipulation is moving people to do what is best for you. Persuasion is moving people to do what is best for them. A mother talking her daughter into finishing school—even though the daughter's boyfriend is telling her that she doesn't need to finish school because he will take care of her—is persuasion, not manipulation.

Convincing a customer to buy a specific product because it has the highest commission rate—even though a different product would better suit his needs—is not persuasion, it is manipulation.

However, urging a customer to purchase from you because you know that the product will meet their needs and your company has the best service in town is not manipulation, it is persuasion, and it is the right thing for your customer. The fact that you get paid to persuade people does not make it any less honorable, what it does do is put responsibility on you to have absolute confidence in every word you say to your customers.

BE A BLESSING

One day Jesus and his disciples were walking along a road in Galilee, an area adjacent to the Sea of Galilee which contains several small towns. Of course, 2000 years ago roads were nothing more that well-traveled dirt paths and travel was done primarily on foot for commoners. It was not uncommon for Jesus and his disciples to walk for hours or even days at a time when they traveled from place to place and this day was no exception. They were on their way to Capernaum, a town with about 1500 people in it. It is sometimes referred to as Jesus' "Own city," not because He was from there, but because it was the center of His ministry. It was a familiar city to the disciples as well, as five of them were from the city itself, or resided nearby.

On this particular day, Jesus and his disciples walked along this familiar dirt road and as they walked, the disciples began to argue with one another. They took care to keep their voices down as they didn't want Jesus to hear them, but they argued nonetheless. Finally they reached the town and entered a house for some much needed shade and rest. Once they were all inside Jesus asked the twelve, "What were you arguing about on the road?" Instead of a response, Jesus only got silence.

The disciples were embarrassed by their conversation that day. They had been arguing about which one of them was the greatest. I imagine they were comparing resumes and recounting all their good deeds to one another, each emphasizing just how important he was to God's kingdom, while downplaying the work of his peers.

Jesus knew exactly what they had been arguing about, of course, so He invited them all to sit down so he could talk to them as a group. Once they were seated, Jesus made a statement that people like me who struggle with their own pride have struggled to swallow for over 2000 years. Jesus said, "Anyone who wants to be first must be the very last, and the servant of all."

Our society that tells us that the key to happiness and success is to do what is best for ourselves. If we just look out for "Number 1," we can get to the top. Jesus and the Word of God tell us something very different. Christ set the example of how to live a life where others come first, and in serving others, God blesses us for our obedience.

With that in mind, below you will see the Blessing Ladder. Each rung of the ladder represents a critical question you must ask yourself every time you are making a sale, starting with the most important question first.

AM I A BLESSING TO GOD?

We often think about how God blesses us. There are multitudes of books dedicated entirely to that subject. As a professional salesperson, what you need to ask yourself is something entirely different. You need to ask if you are being a blessing to Him.

In order to answer that question, we first need to know how we, as mere humans, can be a blessing to God. There are several ways in which we can be a blessing to God, but I want to focus on one. We are a blessing to God when we put the needs of others before our own. Christ himself said, "A new command I give you: Love one another. As I have loved you, so you must love one another. By this everyone will know that you are my disciples, if you love one another."

Jesus was not talking about romantic love or a feeling towards one another. The love He refers to is a love that is defined as identifying the needs of others and then tending to those needs as we are able. For you as a salesperson and expert in your industry, you have the ability to identify the needs of others in a very unique and powerful way, and it is up to you to tend to those needs to the best of your ability by helping the customer choose and buy the product or service that best suits their needs.

It is very important to understand the "Why" in this verse. Jesus clarifies this in the last sentence. He says, "By this everyone will know that you are my disciples, if you love one another." Loving one another is about far more than meeting temporal needs. When we Love one another, we point people toward the ultimate love; the love of God - Jesus. Our witness will be on display for Christ when we put our customer's needs before our own, and in a culture where putting others first is such a rare thing, God will be glorified. Indeed, God will be blessed.

AM I A BLESSING TO MY CUSTOMER?

Being a blessing to your customer means you have to be focused on them. It is not enough to just put your customer's needs first, you must strive to understand what your customer's needs really are.

I remember a time when we had a customer come in and want to purchase marble for a commercial project. The salesperson came to me and asked if he could get a special price on the product for the customer, as it was a large job. The salesman believed that if we did, we would get the order right then.

I walked over to the customer and after I had introduced myself, I said to the customer, "I understand you are interested in a large quantity of this marble and are ready to purchase it if I can lower the price a bit. Is that correct?" The customer told me that I had it correct, so I replied, "Before I do that, can you tell me what you plan to do with this stone?" The customer then went on to describe the new church building they were about to complete and how they had decided that they wanted their parishioners to see something really beautiful when they first walked in the doors to the church, so this was to be the floor in the foyer.

At this, I looked at the salesman and asked if he knew what the customer was using the marble for, and before he could even answer, the customer interrupted and said that he had not told the salesman what it was for, just that he needed a large quantity of the stone he had in his hand. I thanked the customer for telling me that and said, "Are you aware that this is a polished stone and is slippery, especially when wet?" and, "Did you also know that it is a very soft marble and scratches quite easily even when properly sealed and that there is a significant amount of maintenance that must be done to keep it looking nice?"

The customer didn't know any of these things, of course, and that led us to find a stone that was better suited for his application, while still being beautiful. In this case the customer thought he would be blessed by getting a better price, but the true way to bless him was to discover his true needs.

AM I A BLESSING TO MY FAMILY?

Being a breadwinner carries with it much responsibility. Jesus himself said, "Whoever can be trusted with very little can also be trusted with much, and whoever is dishonest with very little will also be dishonest with much." For most of us, our families have either entrusted us to be one of the primary income earners, or the only income earner. This means that the financial future and security of our families rises and falls with us.

What are our responsibilities as an income earner? Before you're tempted to say, "To bring home a paycheck" I want you to stop and think about this question a little more. Let's say you made $40,000 last year. Is your responsibility to your family to make another $40,000 this year or is it to push yourself to be better than you were last year. And, by the way, most of us also hold the title of mother, father, husband or wife. As the bearer of these titles, are not we also responsible for our families' emotional well-being? For some of us, this means making decisions about balancing family time and work time. It also means balancing ministry time as well. While most of us reading this book are called to provide financially for our families, all of us are called to serve the Lord.

AM I A BLESSING TO MY EMPLOYER?

Luis was a good salesman. Every month he would finish in the top twenty percent of the company, and from time to time would have a break out month and sit on the top of the sales report. His sales numbers, however, were not his best attribute. Luis was also reliable.

If there was a job to be done, he would do it, and he wouldn't quit until it was done. You would never catch Luis on a long lunch break or making personal calls on company time. When it was time to work, he would work, and he was always on time and ready to go. As great as his sales were and as comforting as his reliability was, these were still not his best attributes. Luis' true gift to his employer was his attitude. He was nice, he was kind, he was polite, he was honest and he was professional. Everybody liked Luis. Even the competitors liked Luis. Luis' attitude, more than any other attribute, was a blessing to his employer.

Sometimes we get trapped in the lie that tells us that the only way we can be a blessing to our employer is to add to the bottom line. While revenue and profit are important, many of the CEO's I have discussed this issue with would trade some of that profit for a good night's sleep every time.

Paul wrote, "Whatever you do, work at it with all your heart, as working for the Lord, not for human masters." Ultimately, we need to stay focused on Jesus, our true employer. If you stay focused each day on the One who makes your position possible, the side effect of that work ethic will bless your employer.

AM I A BLESSING TO MYSELF?

This is the last rung on the ladder, but it is still an important one. "For I know the plans I have for you," declares the Lord, "plans to prosper you and not to harm you, plans to give you hope and a future."

While this verse is pointing to the ultimate hope of Christ, it also tells us about the heart of the God who knows every little detail about us. As long as you are doing the right things, God can do what every good father wants to do—give His children good things.

The next time you sell something and earn a good commission you can use to better yourself and your family, be thankful to the one who provided it and let it bring you the happiness that it was intended to bring.

CHAPTER 2
WHAT IS SELLING?

WHEN I WAS about eighteen years old, I was working on my in-car training. "In-car training" is exactly what it sounds like; training while you are in the car. Now back in the 1980's, that meant cassette tapes, and I had a bunch of them. I had books on tape from many of the popular sales trainers of the time. I would listen and learn how to overcome objections. I would learn what to say when a customer said "I'm just looking." I would learn from the experts which closing techniques worked the best and then I would practice the things I had learned over and over again.

By this time I had been selling for 4 years, and my in-car training program had served me well. Although I had barely graduated from high school, I was already consistently one of the top salespeople in the company every month. I know what you are thinking, and no, that is not a typo. I started selling when I were 14 years old. I grew up in a family business. In 1978, when I was just seven years old, my dad opened a carpet store in Sacramento, California. I have two older brothers and an older sister. All of us started helping out at the family business at a young age, and I was no exception. I was a big kid and by the time I hit high school, my dad finally relented to my continual requests to become a salesman. So, by the time I was 18 I already had 4 years of experience.

During that era in the retail carpet business, a good salesperson would sell about one out of every four customers and a very good salesperson would close about one in three. I was falling into the latter category and typically my monthly closing percentage would fall between 30 and 35 percent. So here I am, driving down the highway, and one of my in-car sales trainers said something that changed my life forever. With great drama in his voice, he asked "Do you know what selling is?" I thought to myself "Of course I do, what a silly question." But I was shocked to find out that I actually did not know what selling *really* was.

Since this time, I have asked that same question to every salesperson I have trained, and I have heard every imaginable answer. I have heard things like "Matching a customer to a product," and "Providing a solution to a problem." Some have said "Asking questions to determine a customer's needs" or "Explaining features and benefits." And while all of these things are part of the sales process, none of them define what selling truly is. By the way, with the exception of a couple people that had listened to the same trainer I had learned from, and even though I have trained literally hundreds of sales people, many of whom had many decades of experience, no one has ever answered this question correctly.

So I pose the same question to you. What is selling? Before I tell you the answer, I want to tell you this; if you don't read another chapter of this book, the answer to this one question will change your life. It will change your income, it will change your career and it will change your family tree if you learn to do it well. When I heard the answer to this one question, it changed everything for me. Within a week my close rate had doubled. By the end of the first month my close rate was over 75% and after a year I was consistently selling between 80 and 90 percent of the people that walked into our store. Even more exciting is the fact that over the years I have been able to teach it to other salespeople and create teams whose productivity exploded. I remember one team, for example, where we were able to increase our sales by over 500% per year, with only a 25% increase in the number of salespeople, thanks in large part to the answer to that one question; what is selling? Here is the answer:

Selling is the art of reducing a customer's fear of making a mistake.

I want you to think about that for a moment. Think about the last time you made a major purchase yourself. Maybe it was a house or a car or a private school for your kids. Why did you buy *that* house, or *that* car or *that* school? What were you afraid of? Maybe you were afraid that the house wouldn't be big enough for your family. Maybe you were afraid that the car you were considering would break down and be expensive to maintain or that the teachers at the school you were considering wouldn't be able to motivate your child. Have you got it? Do you know what you were afraid of? Now I want you to think about the buying decision you made. Did the salesperson or product or reputation of the company alleviate that fear? I am willing to bet that they did.

Now that you have this powerful piece of information, it is important to start to develop skills around it. As you talk to your customers start asking yourself some questions. Ask yourself "What is my customer afraid of?" and "What would I be afraid of, if I were this customer?" and "What have other customers, like this one, that I have dealt with been afraid of?"

You also need to be paying close attention to the questions and statements your customer is making, as they hold vital clues to understanding your customer's fears. Look for patterns in their conversation. If your customer is asking questions like "Does that option cost extra?" and "Do you offer financing" and "Does this product ever go on sale?" this should be a red flag that your customer may be afraid that they cannot afford the product or service you are discussing with them. Another customer may ask you questions like "Can you give me some referrals?" and "What type of warrantee comes with this service?" and "How long has your company been in business?" These could be indications that this customer is afraid that they will buy the product you're selling from a company that will not stand behind their work or product if something goes wrong.

Sometimes your customer's fears are obvious, and they may even tell you what they are. In other cases, they may be very difficult to figure out, but I promise it will be worth the effort. Many of us have been trained that you don't have to overcome every objection the customer gives you, and normally, that is true. There are, however, certain objections that you must overcome, and these are the ones that are centered on your customer's fear.

I was working with a salesman one day, trying to help him close a large project that he had been working on for quite some time. Charles, the salesman I was helping had a phone appointment with Doug, the customer, and our plan was that I would listen in on the call and assist however I could. After we planned out the call, including the direction we wanted to take the conversation and the outcome we desired, the conversation started and seemed to be going very well. Charles began by restating their earlier "Discovery" (A term will explore later in the book) and Doug confirmed that indeed, the needs identified in their earlier conversation were the "pain points" that he needed to solve. Charles also confirmed that Doug believed that the solution Charles' company could provide would solve the problem. Together, they quantified the dollars attached to Doug's problem and it was substantially more than the cost of the solution. They discussed timelines, and the dates were pleasing to both Charles and Doug. They discussed item after item and everything seemed to be perfect, but time and again, Charles would ask for the order and Doug would not commit to buy. Finally, I thought I knew why Doug would not move forward. I grabbed a notepad and wrote "He has been burned before."

I handed the note to Charles, who considered for a moment and then said. "Doug, can I ask you a question?" Doug said "Of course." The Charles asked "Have you been burned before by a company like ours?" There was silence on the other end of the line for several seconds, and then, in a somewhat somber voice Doug said "Actually Charles, I have, and it cost me a lot of money, even more time and I don't want to go through that again." Charles responded by asking, "Doug, what would it take for you to feel comfortable that I am going to follow through and do what I have promised you?" Over the next couple minutes Charles and Doug dialoged about what it would take for Doug to be less afraid to make a buying decision and Charles ended that call thanking him for his order.

After the call, Charles asked me how I had known that Doug had been burned in the past. We went through the conversation, comment by comment, and I explained how I had known. We discussed tone of voice and words the customer had emphasized, but in the end, it was the years of listening for fear, along with a healthy dose of the Holy Spirit that helped me to understand what Doug was afraid of. It will be the same for you as well. As you practice listening for clues about your customer's fears, they will become more apparent to you. Many times I look back on situations like Doug's and I am greatly encouraged. Charles' company was able to help Doug in a powerful way that he was truly grateful for. Charles' persuasion of Doug to buy was in Doug's best interest, and Charles is the beneficiary of not just a profit, but also the knowledge that he helped someone make their life better. Just as Paul told us in his letter to the church at Philippi, "Do nothing out of selfish ambition or vain conceit. Rather, in humility value others above yourselves, not looking to your own interests but each of you to the interests of the others."

BLOCKS

THE BUILDING BLOCKS OF SELLING WITH POWER

CHAPTER 3
POWERFUL
CONNECTIONS

YOU TALK TO people every day, but do you really connect to them? A wise man once said "People buy from people they like." and he was right, so how do you get people to like you? Martin Luther King, Jr. said "It really boils down to this: that all life is interrelated. We are all caught in an inescapable network of mutuality, tired into a single garment of destiny. Whatever affects one destiny, affects all indirectly." King was right. We are all connected to one another, and we long for that sense of connection, even if we are not aware of our own longing. As professional salespeople, our lively hood depends on our ability to build trust and understanding with our clients, and nothing secures trust as quickly as a sense of connection.

It was Summer time in the Central Valley of California. Before you start thinking of beaches and surfers, let me describe what this part of Northern California is like. It's hot. 105 degree days are not uncommon and the towns are all surrounded with farmland. Foothills that turn into the towering Sierra Nevada Mountains flank the East like a vigilant watchman while the smell of dairy farms is carried on the breeze that winds its way from the Pacific Ocean up the river delta to the valley floor. It's a smell that is instantly familiar for those that call the Valley home and even now oddly reminds me of the place I spent so many years honing my sales skills.

This day was like many others. It was hot. I got out of my car and walked into the showroom of one of the nicest tile stores in the area. They were a great prospect for me. Unfortunately, to date, that is all they were; a prospect. The man who made all the buying decisions had eluded all of my attempts to make a real presentation. Although he had afforded my some degree of professional curtesy, it was clear that he had no intention of buying even a single piece of tile from me. At least not yet.

My persistence had paid off, however, and he had finally relented and told me I could have ten minutes to present my line to him. So here I was. I let the cool air coming out of the vents dry my forehead for a minute (Did I mention it was hot?) and then headed to the office area for my appointment. The receptionist listened to me tell her who I was and then disappeared down a hallway. In a moment she reappeared and said "Down the hall, first door on your left" before resuming her post at her desk. I headed down the hallway and paused at the office door. Mark was on the phone and clearly engaged in a conversation. He half-heartedly looked up at me and motioned for me to come in and sit down, all the while never missing a beat or pausing in the conversation that he clearly considered more important than the one he was about to have with me.

As I sat down, I looked around the room and noticed he had several personal pictures of himself and his family. Most of the pictures were of them enjoying some activity together like camping or being at sporting events, and then one caught my eye. I looked at it closely, inwardly smiling, as if I had just remembered where I had hidden a gold coin.

About that time, Mark hung up the phone. Before I even formerly introduced myself, I pointed at the picture on the wall and said, "Hey, Mark, is that the speedway in Fontana?" "That is exactly where it is," he said, "Have you been there?" I smiled as said "I go down there every year. It looks like that picture must be from '02 based on the paint scheme on Dale Jarret's car." Now Mark was smiling and sitting forward in his chair as well. "You're right, it was 2002. How could you tell that from the picture?" "Well, I think 2003 was the year that they changed the UPS logo to yellow letters on a brown background on the hood of his car, and that logo is brown letters on a white background." "So you are a Jarret fan!" he exclaimed, now genuinely excited. "Well, I'm really a Bobby Labonte fan, but I love all things NASCAR."

About two hours later, we were setting up the delivery details for the display and samples he had ordered and also set a time for me to return and start training his salespeople on the merits of their newest tile line.

So what had happened? Was my being a race fan so important that Mark thought he should buy my tile? Of course not. I was able to break the ice and make a connection with Mark. I was able to establish that we had something in common. We shared a passion for the same sport. There were plenty of other clues that Mark and I had common interests. I could have made a comment about the picture of him and his son fishing, telling him that it reminded me of fishing with my dad when I was a boy. It could have been that we like the same kind of shoes or lived in the same neighborhood. You get the idea.

Learning to establish a connection, make common ground and build rapport is critical if you want to have a successful sales career. If you are in outside sales, be aware of the environment your prospects work in. Look for evidence of what the person cares about and think of how that relates to your life. If you are inside sales, and your customer comes to you, you can still build rapport, even if you don't yet know much about the customer. If you are in the dead of winter in Wisconsin, you might say "Welcome to the snowmobile warehouse. Can you believe how cold it is out there today?" Even something as mundane as the weather can connect people together, so make a connection if you can. Even those folks who make their living making outbound sales calls can still make a connection. Go online, check out the companies' website. Is the office rural or urban? Is it raining where they are? Look for information about your customer, because when they feel you understand them, they are far more receptive to the idea of listening to you.

For many years I traveled the country managing sales teams, so I have intimate knowledge of most states and many cities. On several occasions I have called or met people from Marietta, Georgia, and every time I do, I say the same thing. "Marietta, home of the Big Chicken!" Now that may sound silly to all of you who don't live in Marietta or Atlanta, but I promise you, if someone does live there, they know exactly what I am talking about.

On one of his journeys, the apostle Paul traveled to Athens and went to a place called Mars Hill. At that time and in that place, Greeks would gather there to talk about new ideas. This was the birthplace of philosophy and Paul understood exactly who is audience was. On the day recorded in the Book of Acts, Paul goes to the place where the people were gathered and he tells them this, "Men of Athens, I observe that you are very religious in all respects. For while I was passing through and examining the objects of your worship, I also found an altar with this inscription, 'TO AN UNKNOWN GOD.' Therefore what you worship in ignorance, this I proclaim to you. The God who made the world and all things in it, since He is Lord of heaven and earth, does not dwell in temples made with hands; nor is He served by human hands, as though He needed anything, since He Himself gives to all *people* life and breath and all things; and He made from one *man* every nation of mankind to live on all the face of the earth, having determined *their* appointed times and the boundaries of their habitation, that they would seek God, if perhaps they might grope for Him and find Him, though He is not far from each one of us; for in Him we live and move and exist, as even some of your own poets have said, 'For we also are His children.' Being then the children of God, we ought not to think that the Divine Nature is like gold or silver or stone, an image formed by the art and thought of man. Therefore having overlooked the times of ignorance, God is now declaring to men that all *people* everywhere should repent, because He has fixed a day in which He will judge the world in righteousness through a Man whom He has appointed, having furnished proof to all men by raising Him from the dead."

Paul first made a connection with the Greeks by mentioning one of their own alters. Later he reinforces his connection with them by mentioning their poetry. Neither of these references were on accident. Paul was one of the most educated men of his time, and that combined with the guidance of the Holy Spirit created a powerful ability for Paul to connect with others.

So what was the result? Did Paul make the sale? The answer lies in Acts 17:32-34. "Now when they heard of the resurrection of the dead, some *began* to sneer, but others said, "We shall hear you again concerning this." [33] So Paul went out of their midst. [34] But some men joined him and believed, among whom also were Dionysius the Areopagite and a woman named Damaris and others with them."

Paul made the connection and he made the sale.

CHAPTER 4
RIGHT THING,
WRONG REASONS

AS A SALES manager, I often recommend sales books to
my salespeople. I have a long list of resources that I think
are tremendous and often recommend specific books to
different people based on their particular skillset and needs.
There is one book, however, that is on my list, but almost
never gets mentioned. This book is very well written. It is
engaging and even funny at times. The book is packed with
great techniques ranging from prospecting to closing. The
"Do's" in this book are spot on, but the problem lies in the
"Why." The general message of this book is that you should
use all of the techniques he teaches and say all of the things
he says, because it is what's best for *you*. In the author's eyes,
it's all about taking care of number one; yourself. He would
say let the buyer beware, because you need to take care of
yourself first. If your goal is to be a grifter or a hustler, this
is a good plan, but if you want a sales career, this will lead

you to a dead end and a bad reputation. It will also lead to a broken, disconnected relationship with God and a need for repentance.

A good friend of mine likes to say that sometimes we need to learn to eat the fish and spit out the bones. In other words, we need to absorb the truth and filter out the lies. Every once in a while I will recommend that book to a salesperson, but only if he or she is a mature believer that has a strong relationship to Christ and is able to listen to the Holy Spirit's guidance while reading the book. I know you are trying to figure out which book I am talking about, so I will make you a deal. One day, when you and I are friends, and I am confident in your relationship with God, I will tell you the name of the book.

When it comes to our behavior at work, many of us justify our words and actions because "It is our job," but being a professional salesperson means having absolute integrity. Jesus' half-brother James said "If you really keep the royal law found in Scripture, ""Love your neighbor as yourself,"' you are doing right." I hear many people say things like "There is a fine line between truth and market- ing" and "This is one of the gray areas in sales." Implying that it is okay to exaggerate or even tell a little lie, if it is in name of business.

If James was correct in saying that doing the right thing means loving each other, then how can we possibly justify the idea that lying is acceptable? When James said "Love your neighbor" he was not referring to a feeling. James was referring to love as an action. Love in this case has everything to do with what we say and what we do, regardless of how we feel. If you know someone who has been unpleasant to you, but you see they have a need and you help them anyway, you have loved them. If someone is a close friend and has a need but you do nothing, then you have failed to love them. Keep this in mind as you love your customers. The customer is not always right, but it is always right to love them regardless.

One of the most powerful testimonies you can display to your customers is doing the right thing. People want to do business with honest people that they can trust. Doing the right thing is not only a witness to the customer you are interacting with, it also leaves a powerful impression on your other customers that witness it first or second hand. Sometimes we do the right thing and no one is around. Sometimes we are tempted to think that it was foolish to be completely honest because no one was an eye witness to the event, but remember, God sees everything. God knows you have options. He knows when you choose the high road and He promises to reward us for it. God is the most powerful ally you could possibly have for your business. God will not enter the presence of anything unholy, but when you live your life the way God intended you to, blessing will come like a roaring river into your life.

CHAPTER 5
PERSISTENCE
IS PAINFUL

SOLOMON SAID, "WHOEVER is slothful will not roast his game, but the diligent man will get precious wealth." Few of us use words like slothful these days, so let me paraphrase what the wisest man who ever lived said. If you are lazy and inactive, you will never achieve anything, but if you are persistent and intentional, you will be successful.

So what does it take to be successful in sales? Weather you sell face to face or on the phone, you must be actively pursuing your customers. This seems so simple, yet one of our biggest enemies is call reluctance. We will talk about the "Why's" of call reluctance later, but for now let's simply agree that we all face call reluctance to one degree or another.

So how many calls is enough? To answer that question, we need to work backwards. How many appointments, on average, does it take for you to make a sale? For the sake of this example, let's say that you close one out of every 4 appointments. Next, how many calls does it take for you to get an appointment? Let's say you can turn one out of every five calls into an appointment. Last, how many sales per day do you need to stay on budget? Let's say that you need 2 sales per day to hit your quota. That means that you need 5 (calls per appointment) x 4 (appointments per sale) x 2 (sales per day) = 40 calls per day to reach your quota.

I don't know about you, but I don't just want to hit my quota. I want to crush it. If you want to do the same, then make more than 40 calls per day. Make 60 calls and beat your quota by 50%. Make 80 calls and double your sales. Did you just roll your eyes? Are you thinking "No one could make that many calls" right now? You are wrong. Someone is doing it, and it's likely a competitor. That lady or man that seems to everywhere, taking all your customers... She is making 80 calls per day. Do you want to be better? Do you think God wants you to be better? Do you think He wants you to lead by example and show those around you what a man can do when he has Christ on his side? He wants you win, for His glory, and you get to play a part in the process.

What you need to start considering is "How do I increase my call volume?" First, take the time to analyze how you spend your time. How much time do you spend chatting with your co-workers, taking personal calls, surfing the internet, stopping for coffee, etc.? While there is nothing wrong with any of these activities, they are burning precious selling time during the day. If you want coffee, leave home fifteen minutes early. Stop for gas on the way home from work, not during your precious, limited work time. You get the point. If you have never *really* done an accounting of how you spend your time, you will be shocked at the incredible amount of time that is wasted. Use that time for calls and you will be rewarded.

Next, examine your processes. If you are a traveling salesperson, look at your call routes. Are they efficient? Many salespeople enter their day with some idea of who they plan to see, but end up reacting to phone calls and emails that change their plans and make their travel time very inefficient. Let's say that you have a customer that you need to see once per week. Does that customer have an expectation that they will see you walk in the door every Thursday morning, or are your visits random? It is amazing how conversations change when you create service expectations with your customers. The call that you get right now goes something like this, "Good morning Joe, this is Susie from ABC Supply, I need a sample of that new widget you showed me last time you were here. Can you drop one by this afternoon?" And you respond with, "You bet Susie, I will run by the office and pick one up. I should be able to get it to you by about 2:00 pm." After all, this is your biggest customer, right? You want them to know how much you value their business. Well, frankly, sometimes it is just a huge waste of time. When you have a consistent call plan, you will find the phone call usually goes more like this, "Good morning Joe, this is Susie at ABC Supply. Can you drop by a sample of that new widget you showed me last time you were here when you come in this Thursday?" How much better is that? No special trip to the office, no trip back across town, and your customer still knows how much you value their business because you are professional and consistent.

What about the times when Thursday is not good enough? What if your customer says, "Good morning Joe, This is Susie from ABC Supply. I know you are coming in on Thursday, but I need a sample of that new widget you showed me before then. Can you drop one off this afternoon?" Most of us will immediately respond with a "Yes," drive all over town and think we are the best sales rep ever. Few of us will ask questions like "Susie, thank you for thinking of our new widget, we are all excited about getting them into the market. I am across town right now and don't have one with me. I have one at home that I could bring you in the morning and would be willing to be at your door when you open. Would that be soon enough?" in many cases, it will be. You can make your customer happy and keep selling without wasting half the day in your car.

How we pursue leads will have a dramatic impact on not only our income, but also our reputation. Choose to pursue your work as if Jesus is your sales manager. After all, He is.

CHAPTER 6
KICK UP THE SILT

KYLE IS A great closer. It never failed that following his powerful presentation, he would ask for and receive the order. Sometimes customers would even ask him to write up the sale before Kyle had even asked. Customers love Kyle. I have seen customers invite him to dinner, and drop by the shop, just to say hello. Kyle doesn't just make customers, he makes friends. The joke around the office is that when a customer walks in, Kyle will not only get a sale, he will get a new friend, too.

Like all people, however, Kyle has a weakness. He hates the phone. Kyle would rather work all day in the hot Texas Summer sun for free than make prospecting calls for an hour in an air conditioned office. Kyle and I were training one day because sales at the store Kyle worked at had slowed way down. A combination of bad weather and local economic issues had caused walk in traffic to drop by about 50%. This decline in foot traffic meant that Kyle's sales were cut in half as well.

Kyle and I spent all morning going over ideas that could help improve the stores sales. I knew exactly what the problem was, but I wanted Kyle to come to the realization himself. We talked about marketing ideas and decided that marketing was a long term solution that really wouldn't help us today. We talked about merchandising next. While there were improvements we could make, merchandising really wasn't the problem because we were selling the people that walked in; we just didn't have enough people walking in. Then we talked about the sales process. We discussed presentation, closing, emotional involvement and every aspect of the process you can think of. The conclusion was always the same. While those things are important, they really won't help us now.

Kyle had been skirting the real issue all day. He had avoided the topic at every turn, but as the day wore on, he knew at some point he would have to address it. Exacerbated, Kyle finally looked at me and said, "Ok, you're going to tell me the truth about what I really need to do now, aren't you." I replied, "No, Kyle, I want you to tell me." Kyle sighed and said "What I really need to be doing is following up on the phone with my old customers and the ones that didn't buy, right?" I smiled and said, "Do you think that is the problem?" Kyle said "Yes, my problem is that I am not making my calls." "You are right Kyle. Your problem is that you need to be on the phone making calls, and you need to be making them three months ago."

Kyle's eyes blinked. "Huh?" he said. I went on, "Our average sales cycle is about 90 days. That means if you want a sale today, you need to have made calls three months ago. You can start making calls today, and you should start making calls today, but they will have their biggest impact on your wallet 90 days from now, not today."

Solomon said "A sluggard's appetite is never filled, but the desires of the diligent are fully satisfied." Said another way, "Lazy people want much but get little, but those who work hard will prosper." Pipeline activity is critical for sales success. For some people that means getting on the phone. For some it may mean getting in your car and seeing potential clients. For others it may mean tradeshows or some other event, but regardless of how you stir your pipeline, creating activity with your customers must be done on a constant basis.

Think for a moment about how many people you have sold to since you took your current job. Now, when was the last time you talked to any of them? Are you reaching out to past customers? They are the easiest sale there is! How about folks that you have tried to sell, but missed? How many of them even know you still work at the same company? What about the customers you had at your previous job? Do they know where you work now? I understand that what you sold at your last job may not line up with what you sell now, but what if you end up in that previous industry again? Will you still have been in contact with the people that liked you enough to buy from you before?

Staying connected to a large number of people used to be very hard, but with social media you can stay connected with literally thousands of people with a single click. As I write this book, Facebook, Twitter, Instagram and especially LinkedIn are great ways to connect in a tangible and unobtrusive way with the people you do business with. By the time you are reading this there is sure to be even better ways to connect to others, but the question is this: Are you using these tools? I don't want to hear that you are too old to use social media or that you don't know how. Do you have kids? Do you have grandkids? Do you know someone somewhere without gray hair? If you said yes to any of those questions, then you know someone who can help you connect with social media. Plus, it is a great excuse to spend a little time with someone who you need to spend a little more time with anyway. The apostle Paul said "Love one another with brotherly affection. Outdo one another in showing honor." Telling someone that you care enough about them that you would like to connect with them not only conveys affection, it also shows them honor.

Have ever seen one of those television documentaries on people who scuba dive for sunken treasure? Once they identify the general site of the treasure, they gear up and swim to the bottom of the ocean. The problem is, they can't see the treasure they are searching for. Over the years, dirt, clay and other sediment in the water has settled on top of the ocean floor, covering the waiting treasure under a layer of silt. To uncover the treasure, the divers bring down huge vacuum cleaner looking hoses, and as the diver disturbs the ocean floor, the vacuums pull the silt away, exposing the treasure underneath. Your pipeline is the same way. Hidden inside that list of contacts is buried treasure. That treasure will support your family and bring blessings into your life and the lives of your customers, but the only way to separate the dirt from the gold is to stir up your pipeline. You need to kick up the silt and expose what God has planned for you. I promise it will be more precious than gold or silver.

CHAPTER 7
SELLING IS AN ART;
MAKE IT COLORFUL

CAN YOU REMEMBER anything about the last salesperson that sold you something? In order to stand out among our peers, we must learn to leave an impression that people will remember.

Many years ago I was in the national sales manager role selling building materials. Part of my job was to handle national retail accounts and Berkshire Hathaway owned a company that I had targeted, but had been unsuccessful getting any business from. The crux of my problem was simple; the buyer for national programs would not give me a meeting. I had tried many times unsuccessfully to get an audience even though we had been selling them in a few local markets including the one I used to work in before I was promoted to the national level. The company was building a huge new store in California, and rumor had it that Arnold Schwarzenegger and Warren Buffet were both going to be at the grand opening party. Even more importantly, my elusive buyer was supposed to be there too.

After making a couple of phone calls, I traveled to the west coast to visit my past customer who was now the manager of the new store that the company was opening. Steve, my past customer, was apologetic when we met. He felt bad because I had traveled all the way from Dallas, only for him to deliver the bad news that he wasn't allowed to give any suppliers invitations to the private party without his regional manager's permission. "Steve," I said "would you call your regional manager and ask him to let me attend the party?" Steve replied that as much as he would like to, there was no way he would let me come, because I was not on the "Approved" guest list. So I asked Steve another question, "What could I do for you that would be so helpful that you would help me get into the party?" Steve laughed out loud and then said, "Well, unless you can get your biggest competitor to send me the gorgeous display they promised to have here on time, I can't think of anything." I dug deeper. "What display are you talking about?" Steve went on the tell me that a competitor of mine had promised to ship him their brand new "Super" display in time for the grand opening, but had failed to ship it at all. I had seen the display he was referring to before, and it was very grand and beautiful.

"Steve," I asked "What if I could make you a beautiful custom vignette, complete with grouted panels and decorative glass?" Steve was listening now, but said "That would be great, but how could you do that in less than 24 hours?" I asked him again "Steve, if I could pull it off, could you get me an invitation?" Steve pulled out his cell phone, dialing as he walked away, obviously calling his regional manager. After a minute or so of animated conversation, Steve walked back over to me. "If you can have something beautiful in this empty spot on my showroom by tomorrow morning, I will get you an invitation to the event."

An hour later, four people, including myself were wearing jeans and t-shirts in the warehouse of our distribution center with lumber and everything we needed to build a custom display. While it was a late night to be certain, the next morning when Steve arrived at his store, one of our delivery trucks was waiting for him, and I had my way in.

That evening I was at one of the nicest parties I had ever seen for a store dedication. I arrived too late to see the "Terminator" give his speech, but as I stood in the buffet line admiring the lavish display in front of me, I looked up to see Warren Buffet standing across from me, and the only thing separating us was a tray of chocolate dipped strawberries. "Boy, they sure look good, don't they?" I said to Buffet, referring to the fruit between us. "They sure do." He said as he got one and moved on down the buffet line.

At this point you might be saying to yourself "So you had the chance to ask one of the greatest businessmen who ever lived a question, and you asked him about strawberries?" Well, frankly, yes. But in my defense, I was not there to see Warren Buffet, I was there to see one of his employees, and just a few moments later, I saw him. He was engaged in a conversation with someone and I slyly took up a position where I could watch him. I wanted to approach him alone, so I needed to find the right opportunity. He moved from conversation to conversation and then I saw my chance. He was heading for the door and into a hallway. The hallway, it turned out, was the way to the restroom, which was where he was heading. As he headed down the deserted hallway, I called out "James, may I talk to you for a moment?" He turned around, clearly not knowing who I was. As I approached, I introduced myself. "Hello James, my name is John Kimmel, and I have been trying, unsuccessfully to reach you at your office." As I spoke, recognition flashed in his eyes. James said "You are the guy who has been calling me trying to get an appointment for weeks, and won't give up." I smiled and said "Yes sir, that's me." James paused and then said "How did you get in here?" So I told him how my team stayed up all night building a display that got the local and regional managers out of a jam and how I traded that for an invitation to the event. James thought for a moment and said, "So you did all that just to come to a party with Warren Buffet?" "No," I said, "I did it to come to a party with you. I did it so I could meet you face to face and ask you to give me an appointment to come to your office and let me give you a presentation." James smiled and said "Well, John, no one has ever tried that approach before! I tell you what; this week when you call my office, my assistant will schedule an appointment to come give me a presentation. Now, if you will excuse me, I need to use the restroom." And he turned and walked through the bathroom door.

I am not suggesting that you need to work all night and spend thousands of dollars just to get every appointment, but I tell that story to make a point. I got through to the buyer because I was different. What are you doing to distinguish yourself from all of the other people trying to sell your customers the same product you are selling? Start asking yourself "What can I do to make people remember me?" If all your competitors bring their customers donuts, then bring bagels and cream cheese. If regular business cards are the norm for your competitors then make yours on 3x5 cards. The point is, be different and be creative. Maybe it is something you say. I know salespeople that have voicemails that sound like this, "Thank you for calling Susan Smith at Vintage Motors, make sure you ask me about the candy apple red '67 stingray we just put in the showroom when

I call you back…" Would you remember a voicemail like that one? I'll bet you would, simply because it is different.

God chose to make His creation with incredible creativity and imagination. How creative was God when He created Niagara Falls or the Grand Canyon? Once you have seen sights like those, you will never forget them. Remember, you were created in God's image, so use that creativity to create a memory that your customers will not be able to forget.

CHAPTER 8
GET ANYTHING
YOU WANT

I GOT A call one day from Don, who is someone very close to me. He was distraught. In fact, I had never heard him sound worse and he was having a spiritual crisis of epic proportions. Just a few days earlier, Don had lost one of his best friends, Chuck, to cancer, but it was not the loss of Chuck's physical body that had Don so upset. It was losing Chuck's soul that was the issue.

Don and Chuck had known each other for decades. Don was already a believer when he met Chuck and did his best to love him and encourage him to seek Christ. Don had also waged a spiritual battle from his knees on Chuck's behalf, praying for him daily. Don continued this battle for more than two decades and he believed that his prayers would make a difference. When Chuck was diagnosed with cancer, Don thought surely this would be the catalyst that would bring Chuck to the foot of the cross. Don had heard many stories about how a negative event in our lives can help us to open our eyes to the Truth, and thought surely this is what would happen to Chuck.

Don continued to pray for Chuck, believing that he would be saved and claiming the verses that are written about prayer in the bible, as he understood them. One of those verses was John 15:7 which says "If you remain in me and my words remain in you, ask whatever you wish, and it will be done for you." Chuck, oblivious to the spiritual battle being waged for his soul, however, was getting no closer to Christ. In fact, Chuck's health was failing. As Chuck got closer and closer to death, Don prayed for him even more fervently. Don had heard stories about people that accepted Christ on their deathbed and so believed that a last minute conversion must be God's plan for Chuck.

As Chuck's days came to a close, Don spent time with him every day. Each day Don would tell chuck that Jesus loved him and that He desired a relationship with Chuck. Chuck continued to reply that he did not believe in God. Now in hospice, Don was told one day that this day would almost certainly be Chuck's last. Don realized that today was Chuck's last opportunity for salvation and was determined to make the most of it. As Don visited Chuck for the last time, he didn't waste a moment. He prayed over Chuck. He witnessed as fervently as he ever had in his life to his friend, pleading with Chuck to make the only decision that could save his own life. Chuck listened. He let Don say everything that he wanted to say. When Don was finished, Chuck smiled at his friend. Chuck said "It means a lot to me to hear the words that you said, because I know how much you care about me. I also know that you believe every word that you said Don, but I don't believe in God." And then Chuck was gone and the Devil had won.

Don was devastated. How could this be? Don had asked faithfully for Chuck's salvation. He had believed that God could and would deliver Chuck. Don knew the Bible said that it is God's will that all men should come to Christ, so how could this be? By the time Don and I were on the phone together, Don was in a very dark place. For Don, this prayer not being answered didn't line up to his understanding of the Bible. Don's line of thinking grew more and more poisonous as he told himself that since Chuck was not saved, the Bible must be wrong. Worse, if the Bible was wrong then surely God was not real.

Up to this point, Don had not lived an easy life. He had already endured tragedies and heartbreaks. He had already battled inner demons and experienced the evil effects that Satan has on those around us. As Don was telling me this story, he finally told me the real reason for his call. If God was not real, then there was no reason to stay on this Earth. "There is too much pain here and if there is no God then soon my children and those who love me will be dead also. None of our lives have meaning. I don't want to stay." Now I was the one who was reeling. I stopped to pray. "God," I pleaded. "I need the words to say. Help me now."

The next thing I knew, I was speaking again. "Don, I remember when I was I child, even before I had faith of my own, I used to pray a certain prayer. I would pray that everyone on Earth would be saved and that no one would go to Hell. Did you ever pray a prayer like that?" Don said that he had done the same when he was a child. Then I asked him, "Don, we both know that I didn't actually become born again until I was an adult, but if I had been a believer at the time, would it have made a difference? Would everyone have gone to Heaven if I had believed?" Don replied "Well, of course not." I continued, "But if God gives us anything we want, as long as we believe, and it is in His will, then shouldn't He answer that prayer? You just told me that the Bible says that it is His will that all should come to know the love of Christ. Knowing all of that, you said that "Of course," God would not answer that prayer. Why did you say that?" Don was thinking now. "I never thought about that before. I'm sure that some will not go to Heaven, but how is that so if God wants everyone to go to Heaven?" Don's faith was rising in him as he spoke, trying to reconcile the death of his friend, his unanswered prayer and the Word that Don had always believed was true.

"The reason that Chuck didn't accept Christ was that God has given us all the free will to choose the grace of salvation. God didn't want robots. He wanted us to choose to follow His son." I said and went on, "God never forces us to believe. He presents us the opportunity to believe. He presents us the evidence of His deity. He loves us and pursues us, but he never forces us. We have to make our own choice." Don spoke now, "Then I was just wasting my time all these years. I was praying for something that was not going to happen anyway." "No, Don, think about it. God gave Chuck chance after chance to accept Jesus. You just told me that you witnessed to him over and over, even on his deathbed. God honored your prayer by giving Chuck repeated opportunities to speak to him. God loved Chuck and he loves you. Without your prayers, Chuck may have run out of time long ago."

There are many verses in the Bible that talk about the awesome power of prayer, but do any of them have to do with our careers or making sales? Let's take a closer look at some of these verses.

Matthew 21:22

"And whatever you ask in prayer, you will receive, if you have faith."

Mark 11:24

"Therefore I tell you, whatever you ask in prayer, believe that you have received it, and it will be yours."

John 14:13-14

"Whatever you ask in my name, this I will do, that the Father may be glorified in the Son. If you ask me anything in my name, I will do it."

Matthew 7:7

"Ask, and it will be given to you seek, and you will find; knock, and it will be opened to you."

All four of these verses have some important things in common, and before we go any further it is critical that we understand a few things because these verses are some of the most misunderstood, misquoted verses of the Bible. There are many people who claim that these verses are saying that God will answer *every* prayer and that if a prayer is not answered, then it means you don't have enough faith. These fallacies are tragic and can be devastating for those who believe them.

To understand these verses, we must first understand the matter of the prayer aligning with God's will. Paul the Apostle writes of his own prayer in 2 Corinthians 7-9.

"…Therefore, in order to keep me from becoming conceited, I was given a thorn in my flesh, a messenger of Satan, to torment me. [8] Three times I pleaded with the Lord to take it away from me. [9] But he said to me, "My grace is sufficient for you, for my power is made perfect in weakness." Therefore I will boast all the more gladly about my weaknesses, so that Christ's power may rest on me."

This is a clear example of a believer who is full of faith asking earnestly in prayer for something and the Lord's response is not to grant his prayer. As much as we would like to think that the Lord's first priority is our happiness, the truth of the matter is that He is much more concerned about our holiness. In Paul's case, God explains that it is better for Paul to have this pain in his life so that Paul will remember that his power comes from God, and not from himself.

In order for a prayer to be answered, it must meet specific criteria. First, we must have faith that God is who he says He is and that He is able. Second, we must actually ask. Wanting something is not enough, God wants us to humble ourselves, acknowledge He who has the power, and ask. Third, it needs to bring God glory, even if we are the only ones who know that God has provided for us. Fourth, it must be in God's will. God's perfect plan is not only perfect for Him, it is also perfect for us. God knew that Paul would be a better witness if his prayer was not granted. Remember, God wants to bless those who live for Him. He only says "No" when that is the answer that is best for us.

CHAPTER 9
POWERFUL CLOSING

I WAS ONLY nineteen years old. I had been selling flooring for about five years in our family owned store and was
doing a house call for a customer that had been in our store
earlier in the week. Darrell had chosen a pattern matched
berber that was all the rage in the late 1980's. It was one
of our best sellers. While Darrell checked the color he had
chosen against his paint and furniture, I went about measuring the house. After I finished measuring, I confirmed
that he still loved the color he had chosen and got to work
calculating the cost of the job and writing out an invoice.
I always assume the customer is going to move forward, so
I never write an estimate. Always an order.

Darrell's living room had two couches facing each other
with a coffee table in between. It was clear this man was
more interested in an evening filled with good conversation
than watching TV, as the room was void of a set. We were
sitting opposite one another as I wrote the invoice, using
the coffee table as a writing desk. Behind Darrell on the

wall was a painting of a stream traversing some flowered countryside and behind me was the doorway leading back into the kitchen.

As I penned in the form, we discussed delivery date, installation details and other essential information. Darrell had made a request when he was in the store. He said that he didn't want to haggle over the price, so if I would give him my best price right from the start, he would appreciate it. Remembering that detail, I did exactly that. Having worked out all of the other issues, it was now time to present the price and get the order.

Smiling, I slid the form across the table toward Darrell. Darrell's eyes made their way to the bottom of the form and as he read, his face looked as if he had just received surprise divorce papers. He almost seemed to be in pain. "Wow, that much?" was all he said, rereading the paper as if he couldn't believe his eyes. I said nothing. After a moment, he looked at me and said, "So what is the very best you can do on this price?" I reminded Darrell of his earlier request and let him know that the price on the invoice was the best price I would do.

To be clear, the price I had quoted Darrel really was the best I would do. It was also the best price Darrell was going to find anywhere. We stocked that particular product by the truckload and were substantially less expensive than our competitors already. I had given him an additional discount and we had some of the best carpet layers in the city. Our company was the leading store in Sacramento and I knew this was the best decision Darrell could make.

After a bit of theatrical hemming and hawing on Darrell's part, I asked him a couple of questions. "Do you love this fabric and color? Darrell said that he did. "As we discussed, this is a very durable product, can you see yourself living with it for a long time?" Again, Darrell affirmed my question. "Then why don't you take it?" I asked. Darrell looked at me, then down at the invoice. As he raised his head back up to me, his face looked conflicted. It was if he was on the edge of a precipice. It seemed like the lightest breeze would push him over the edge and send him reaching for his checkbook.

With a head full of Zig Ziglar, Brian Tracy and others I had been reading, I knew exactly what I should do. I kept my mouth shut and said nothing. Darrell's face went dark, and my gut told me I was about to lose the sale, but still, I said nothing. Over the next several minutes, Darrell's face changed expressions as he seemed to be on a roller coaster of emotions. Occasionally, he would glance past me, as if he was looking at something in the kitchen then set his gaze back on me. I would occasionally look past Darrell to the painting of the stream, thinking how nice it would be to sitting under a tree in that painter's vision. In fact, I would have preferred to be just about anywhere other than on that couch as the silence kept going longer and longer. I could feel sweat on my brow. I could feel the tension in the air. While I just wanted to jump up and say "Fine, you win, I will cut the price!" but knew that would not result in a sale. I had to be firm, so I sat there smiling as it seemed an eternity past with not a word exchanged between us.

Finally, mercifully, Darrel spoke. With a deep sigh, he said "Ok, I will take it." I let out a sigh of my own and handed him my pen. As he signed the paperwork and wrote me a check I asked, Darrell, what do you do for a living?" He smiled as he said "I am the National Sales Trainer for Subaru." I laughed and then asked, "So how did I do?" Darrell smiled as he replied, "You did great. I decided to buy from you before you got here, but once I saw you had some formal sales training, I wanted to test you. You just set the record for longest pause using the "Silence Close."

"It seemed like forever. How long was it?" I asked. At that, Darrell pointed toward the kitchen. Confused, I looked that direction and then noticed the clock above the doorway. As I turned back to Darrell, he said "Fifteen minutes. Well done. I would ask you if you are interested in selling cars, but I have a feeling you are happy where you are." I confirmed that I was very happy where I was, thanked him for the order and headed out the door.

While there are many proven techniques you should use to close the sale, it is most important to remember a couple of things. First, closing is not something you do to someone, it is something you do *for* someone. Many people struggle to make decisions even if they are good ones. Part of your job as a professional salesperson is to persuade the customer to make the best decision possible. Second, many salespeople, especially those new to sales, are daunted by the term "Closing." Closing is simply a term that means asking for the order. I love the way Zig Ziglar used to put it. When Zig would talk about the sales process and getting to the close, he would say that "until you close the sale, you are just a professional conversationalist." His statement is right on. There are literally millions of professional conversationalists out there. Repeatedly, research shows that more than half of the sales presentations made end with no attempt to close. This is especially troubling in light of the fact that most customers need to be asked to buy more than once before they buy. Set yourself apart and ask for the order.

The real key to great closing is in the sales process before you get to the close. By the time you get to the close, you and your customer should be well versed in the following:

- What the customer wants
- What the customer needs
- What the customer fears and have overcome that fear

- One or more pain points
- Monetary and/or emotional cost of their pain
- How you can help them
- Made an emotional connection between customer and solution
- Made a logical connection between customer and solution

If you and your customer have all of this information and your customer understands it, then persuading them to buy will be easy. If, however, you are missing any of these pieces, your job will be infinitely harder. At this point in my career, most of the sales closes I use are as simple as "How would you like to pay for that?" I don't close every sale, of course, and usually when I miss one, I can track it back to the place where I dropped the ball before I got to the close.

Some customers are easy to read during the sales process. Their body language and tone of voice are clear indicators of how you are doing and how likely they are to buy. Those are the easy ones. Many folks, however, are not so easy to read. Some folks keep their feelings hidden, as if they are in the World Series of Poker with a million dollars in the pot, hoping you cannot tell that they are interested in making a buying decision. When you encounter these customers, it is important to use "Trial Closes" along the way. A trial close is simply a quick reading of your customer's buying temperature. Usually, they look something like "What do you think so far?" or "Does that sound good to you?" They often times are specific to the product you are selling as well. If you selling Men's suits, you might ask "How is that color for you?" or "Can you see yourself in this jacket?" If you continue to get green lights throughout your sales presentation, you are likely in good shape when you get to the close.

Many sales closes that you read about are really an objection handling tool, morphed into a sales close. Many of them work quite well, but in most cases, they only are successful when done flawlessly. An example of this would be the "Feel Felt Found Close." This close is used when you think you are dealing with the only objection standing between you and a sale. Let's say you are selling investments and your customer is a first time investor and is afraid they will lose their nest egg. The "Feel Felt Found" close would sound like this:

Customer: "I really need to go home and think about this, I don't know how I would sleep at night if I made a mistake."

Salesperson: "I know exactly how you feel. In fact, many of our first time clients felt the same way before they started growing their nest egg with our firm. What they found, however, was that after they made wise investments and their retirement began to grow, it gave them piece of mind unlike any they had experienced before. Why don't you go ahead and make your investment now so we can start growing your money immediately."

Done perfectly, this close can be very effective, but beware – done poorly, this close sounds "salesy" and can hurt the outcome of your sales presentation. I prefer to use the "Feel Felt Found" tool to handle objections, but I do not combine it with a close.

My advice: Focus on getting all of the other steps in the sales process correct and keep the close simple and direct. Once you are rocking it every month and every year, then you can add more complicated closing techniques to your sales arsenal. If you are already there, I will give you more closing techniques on my website:

www.JohnJKimmel.com

BLUEPRINT

THE PLAN THAT TIES
IT ALL TOGETHER

CHAPTER 10
SALES CALL G.P.S.

IF I NEED to get somewhere, I simply pull out my phone and get detailed directions. You may only get one shot at selling that next customer, so you had better know the directions to the place you want to go. The problem is that most salespeople hate processes, and no one dislikes process more than I do. If you look at my DISC profile, my Strengths-Finder profile or any other personality driven test I have ever taken, it is clear that I am not a man who is naturally predisposed to doing things in a particular order. If you happen to have the most common personality traits of a successful salesperson, you can relate to what I am saying. Many of us live our lives in random order, not necessarily stopping at point B, just because we are traveling from A to C. This lifestyle serves us well in many ways and keeps our days varied and interesting. Unfortunately, there is a problem. If we apply this same haphazard pattern to our selling, we will fail.

Some of you will read this chapter of the book and say to yourselves "John is completely wrong. I don't do any of this, at least not in any particular order, and I am doing very well in my career." If that is you, then I have great news; you could be great, maybe even one of the best. Applying these processes to the way you sell will have a huge impact on your success. You might move from struggling to success or from good to great, so pull up those boot straps, suck it up and hang on, because this part is not optional.

STEP ONE: PROSPECTING (OPTIONAL?)

There are a few of you reading this book that work for a company that supplies 100% of your leads and customers. If that is you, this step might be optional. If you work for a company that expects you to find your own customers, even one percent of the time, than this step is not optional. By the way, if you are one of the few smiling right now because your company gives you all your leads, I want you to read this step anyway and the next time you are with your boss, ask them if it is ok for you to add to your own pipeline by doing some extra work to generate extra leads.

When I was a sales rep in the carpet industry, I would often be given new territory to cover, and I always handled it the same way. Early in the morning, I would go to a phone booth and look in the yellow pages to make sure I had a list of every carpet store in town. This was long before the internet and Google. Once I had a complete list of stores, I would map them out and drive to every single one of them before they opened. Most times I could tell by looking at the building, in the windows at their product line and the general appearance of the store, who might be the best fit for my product line.

After canvasing every store in town, I would then drop in to each one that was a potential fit, starting with the one that I thought was the best fit. I would start by talking to the salespeople in front to make sure I understood the client base of the company and other pertinent information. I would also ask them a question. "If your store decides to carry my product line, what other store in town would be a good fit for my line and what stores should I stay away from?" It was very rare that anyone would tell me another store that would be a good fit, but they always tell me the store "To stay away from." The store to stay away from always fell into one of two categories. Either they were the unscrupulous store in town, or more likely, they were the strongest store in town. If I heard over and over that I should stay away from Jimmy's Carpet Barn, then I made sure I had them high on the list of prospects, because Jimmy was likely selling more carpet than anyone else in the area.

The point of this prospecting technique is simple. Work hard to get the best customer you possibly can first. We will talk more in the book about how much time we should spend focusing on "A," "B" and "C" customers, but make sure you start with the folks who are likely to be the very best fit. Today with the proliferation of websites on the internet, we often don't need to get into our cars to learn about our potential customers. For those of you that prospect on your phone or internet from your desk chair, the premise is the same; Focus on the most likely person or company to be a great company first, and work them in order of importance. I have seen many salespeople exclude a great customer because they chose to do business with the wrong company first. Even if you can have an unlimited number of customers in an area, spend your time as wisely as possible, and this means being smart about your prospecting priorities.

STEP TWO: INTRODUCTION

Elaine and Joe are members of Lake Pointe Church where I teach a Life Group class. That is what our church calls what most of you know as Sunday school. Elaine and Joe had made an important decision to find a Life Group and get more plugged in to the church, and on this Sunday morning they found themselves reading the list of Life Groups available. They decided on a class that seemed to fit their age and season of life, which was married couples in their forties with teenagers.

After consulting their map, they headed for the classroom, which was in another part of the building. On their way there, they passed by a classroom and stopped. Obviously, someone must have said something funny, because laughter filled the classroom and poured out into the hallway gabbing the attention of Joe and Elaine both. The couple looked at each other. Elaine said "They sure sound like they are having fun in there." Joe responded by consulting his class list again and said, "This class is also married couples in their forties with teens. Should we try this class instead?" Elaine smiled and nodded her approval and they entered the classroom.

Joe and Elaine have been members of our class ever since that day and it is one of my favorite stories about how God brings families together in Life Group. God knew that Joe and Elaine would respond to a certain environment and His divine intervention led to a powerful first impression.

Think about it for a moment. You had developed an opinion about whether you would enjoy this chapter just by reading the title. First impressions are powerful and not easily overcome. Phil McAleer, a psychologist at the University of Glasgow in Scotland has done research which concludes that people form strong impressions with as little as a single word being spoken. For those of you who do selling on the phone, that means that if you start your call the wrong way, your entire call will be an uphill battle. Have you ever placed a call and then become distracted before the person you are calling answers? The person then answers the phone and you are jolted back to the reality of your task at hand, and find yourself fumbling for what to say. Tone of voice matters, and in this case, your confusion and lack of confidence and timing are like a poison dart to your sales call, conveying the message that you don't care about the person you are calling and creating an environment of distrust.

My sales career was responsible for my family and I having to move more than a dozen times in as many years of marriage. In 2003, my career moved me to the South for the first time, and I found myself in Little Rock, Arkansas. Here I was, this young, hot-shot salesman and sales manager from California, ready to show all of my new salespeople how to take their careers to the next level. My job was simple. Manage the sales team and lead by example on the sales floor. There was only one problem; no one would buy from me. For almost a month, I helped customer after customer, and no one would buy a thing.

I was frustrated and even started to second guess my move to Arkansas when I got some sage advice from Cliff, one of the cagey older salespeople in the company. He knew why I wasn't making sales. Actually, everyone knew, except me.

One day, seeing I was frustrated and having some empathy, Cliff pulled me aside. He said "John, you know none of us wanted some kid from California telling us what to do, which is why no one has told you what your problem is. But you have been here a while now, and I think you're a good kid, so I'm gonna tell you. You sound like a Yankee, and no one here trusts a Yankee." To be honest, at this point, I was not even sure I knew what a Yankee was, but this is what I found out; if you are in the South, but you are not *from* the South, you are a Yankee. They say that people from the West Coast have no accent, but to the folks in Arkansas, my accent was as plain as day, and it created an environment of distrust. That was the day I learned to speak with a southern accent.

Fast forward to today and I have lived in the South for more than a decade, mostly in the great state of Texas. My natural speaking voice has a little twang to it and I commonly use words like "Y'all" and phrases like "fixen' to," as in, "Are Y'all fixen' to come by after church?" By the way, my spell checker is telling me that both those words are misspelled. Even though I do speak with an accent, because I grew up out West, I can easily turn it off when I wish to. My experience in Arkansas taught me a valuable lesson, and it has served me well. Today, if I am calling a customer in the North East, West or Mid-West, I intentionally turn my accent off. If I am calling someone in Alabama, however, I let my now natural accent fly.

I am also semi-literate in Spanish. I call it Spanglish. Although my vocabulary is weak, I get comments all the time from Spanish speakers that I speak Spanish well. The reason is that I have worked hard to develop my Spanish accent and really try to say the words correctly. When you take the time to speak in a way that is comfortable to the person you are speaking with, it shows them honor. If you are speaking with someone formal, speak formally. If they speak casually, you should speak casually. The apostle Paul was a master at establishing rapport with his audience before he would introduce them to the Gospel. If his audience was a group of Greek philosophers, then Paul would speak in formal Greek. If they were Hebrew peasants, then his language and style would adjust accordingly.

You have also likely heard the saying "You only have three seconds to make a first impression." Is that true? Do you really only have three seconds? According to Eric Wargo, an expert on the subject, research indicates that the actual time you have to create the first impression is 0.1 seconds. For those of you who sell face to face, that means that by the time the customer has walked in and laid eyes on you, they have already formed an opinion, even before you have said a single word. Your dress, facial expression, posture and attention all attribute to that impression. All of that to say this; be prepared for your audience before they arrive, it will have an enormous impact on your sales.

Many of you are in retail so I want to take the time to discuss making an introduction in a retail environment. I cut my teeth in sales as a retail flooring salesman. Like most rookies, when I first started, my introduction would go something like this, "Good afternoon, may I help you find something today?" The customer would reply "No, thanks, we are just looking." I would then sulk back to my desk, hope they found something they were interested in and miraculously find their way back to me. I need to point something out. I worked at a retail flooring store. We sold carpet and vinyl. Never, indeed not one time in the history of the world, has anyone driven by a flooring store and said, "Hey, let's go look at flooring" if they were not, in fact, in need or want of new flooring. When the customers would say "Just looking" they could have said "Just lying." They were shopping, not looking. If you are telling yourself "Those people were just tire kickers and they weren't really in the market to buy," stop saying that right now. What you should be telling yourself is "This person is in the market to buy what I sell. Our company is the best place for them to buy, and I am the best salesperson to make sure that this customer does not make a mistake in their buying decision.

The best way to help them is to make sure they buy from me." If any part of that statement does not ring true for you, go back to the beginning of this book and start over. Integrity is critical to your success, and if you don't believe the best thing your customer can do is buy from you, then you will struggle with everything else.

When a retail customer walks in your store, do not pounce on them. Your job is to help them, not intimidate them. Let your customer come in and orient themselves on something you sell. If they do make eye contact with you, then you should make eye contact and smile back. If they continue eye contact, then you should approach, if not, give them a moment to scan your store. Letting them fix on a product category will help you know what your opening line should be.

Customers are conditioned to try to get rid of you, even if they really need your help. Because of this, do not give a yes or no question that allows them to shed your assistance quickly. If you say, "Can I help you find something?" the customers predetermined response will be "No, thank you, we are just looking." Instead ask them a multiple choice question. For example, if you work in an appliance store, after seeing them eyeing the refrigerators, you might say, "Good afternoon, were you looking for a refrigerator or perhaps a dishwasher today?" Usually, you will get a response indicating what they are after, even if it is something different. The customer might say "Actually, I noticed how nice those new refrigerators look, but I actually need a new dryer."

Often, you will get a second push back at this point. Remember, the customer is conditioned to try to get rid of you. You know that you have their best interest in mind, but they do not know that yet. A common response to the first "refrigerator or dishwasher" question might sound something like this, "We are thinking about a new refrigerator, but we are just looking." Most salespeople then say "Ok, the fridges are over there, let me know if you have any questions," but not you. You are a professional salesperson that is an expert on your product and you know that the best way to help your customer is to stay with them and guide them through this process. When your customer says, "We are thinking about a new refrigerator, but we are just looking." You should smile and say "Fantastic, we have a great selection to choose from." As you are saying this, turn toward the products in question and start walking in that direction. As you are walking toward the refrigerators, say "Let me show you how the department is organized. We have the refrigerators organized by price with the less expensive models to your left and the ones with more features to your right. Were you looking for a white or stainless steel finish?" At this point very few people will repeat the request to be left alone as they realize that they are talking to a professional who can truly help them with what they need. You also have asked them two important questions. You now know what appliance they need and the finish they desire. As you will learn in the following sections, a great salesperson asks a lot of questions.

For most salespeople, especially those in retail or who take inbound calls, the introduction stops here and the process moves to "Discovery." However, if your sales process includes cold calls, either in person or on the phone, then there is one more step. Before you can move to presentation, you need to justify the idea that spending time with you is in the customer's best interest.

The key to getting someone to stay on the phone long enough to learn about them is to offer them value. If you call up and say, "Hello Mrs. Customer, I am calling to tell you about my business," What is in it for them? Most of us make the mistake of thinking "If I can keep talking and keep my prospect on the phone, I have a better chance to sell them something." Nothing could be further from the truth. Keeping someone on the phone for two minutes while you launch into a presentation is not going to persuade the customer to buy anything. In fact, it's annoying, or worse. What you need to do is offer them value, and you need to do it fast. I am going to give you a couple of examples of how to do that.

Tom Latourette is a good friend of mine and he is also a partner at M3 Learning. Tom teaches what he calls the 30 second speech and it is broken into three pieces. The first section of your speech is about you. Introduce yourself, your company and let your customer know what you do. Sounds simple right? Well, there is a catch. You need to accomplish that in 10 seconds or less. I will give you an example in a moment of what that looks like. The second section consists of two or three ways you can potentially help your customer stated in the form of questions. Like the first section, you have about ten seconds to accomplish your goal. The third section is connecting to your customer and flipping the conversation back into their court, to begin a dialog. Again, ten seconds or less.

So let's see what this looks like. Jessica is a salesperson at ABC Printing. ABC Printing specializes in high quality print work, locally in the Charlotte, North Carolina area, delivered within 24 hours of the time of order. ABC is not known for price, they specialize in quality and service. Jessica's 30 second speech could go like this:

Good morning, this is Jessica from ABC Printing. ABC specializes in high quality printing right here in Charlotte. My customers regularly ask me questions like "How can I improve the quality of my print graphics?" And "How can I get my order done very quickly?" or "Can a local company provide me better service than one of the national printers?"

These are all great questions, Mr. Customer, but I would like to know about your business. What printing challenges are you seeing right now?

When I read that 30 second speech in a professional, conversational speed, it takes me twenty seven seconds. The second section is a little over ten seconds, but that is okay, as long as the total time is less than thirty seconds. Let's examine what has been accomplished by using this technique. In less than thirty seconds you have told the customer who you are, the name of your company, your company's service area, three distinct advantages to using your company, shown interest in your customer and asked your first question. This method provides the customer several specific reasons that staying on the call would be of value to them, which is your objective at this stage of the call. Remember, when you pick up the phone to make a cold call, you already know that you can truly help your customer, but your customer does not know that yet.

The thirty second speech works great on cold calls where the customer does not know you or your company. Sometimes, however, that is not the case. Sometimes the customer does know your company, maybe they have even been a customer in the past. Let's use the example of Jessica and ABC Printing again. This time, let's assume that Jessica is the latest in the line of salespeople that have reached out to this customer. In fact, let's say that Jessica has been calling this prospect for over a year and has finally gotten the customer to take her call. I call this the "I don't want to bug you call," and it goes like this:

Good morning, Mr. Customer, this is Jessica from ABC Printing. Thank you for taking my call, I really appreciate it. ABC printing specializes in several different types of printing, but since I have never had the opportunity to talk with you and learn about your company, I'm not sure which of the services we offer could be a potential fit. If there is a potential for us to do business together, I would love for both of us to know about it. I also don't want to bug you about things that are not a fit. Are you currently using a high quality print company that offers twenty four hour local delivery service?

Chances are, the salesperson calling before Jessica never showed any empathy or added value to this prospect. Even the idea of "Not being bugged" by a salesperson offers value. This introduction establishes the idea that you actually care about your customer's precious time, and then goes on to give them other business reasons to stay on the call as well. You will notice that this introduction is also just under thirty seconds. Research says that if you keep your opening to under thirty seconds, your chances of success are markedly higher, so keep it under the thirty second mark.

STEP THREE: DISCOVERY

Every step of this process is the most important step in the process. If you are in the introduction step of the sales process, then the introduction is what you need to focus on. You should not be thinking about closing when you are in discovery. By the time you reach discovery, you have already invested valuable time prospecting and making the perfect introduction, so discovery becomes the most important part of the process for you.

Discovery is exactly what it sounds like. This is the part of the sale where you ask a lot of questions in order to determine some very specific and important information.

Matthew records a conversation between Jesus and the Pharisees one Sabbath day. The Pharisees followed Jesus and his disciples through a grain field and on to a synagogue where Jesus healed a man with a withered hand. Realizing that Jesus intended to heal the man, the Pharisees questioned Jesus about his impending behavior, implying that Jesus would be committing a sin by healing the man on the Sabbath day. Jesus retorted, "Which of you who has a sheep that falls into a pit on the Sabbath will not take hold of it and lift it out?"

Jesus was asking a question that appealed to people's logic. Specifically, logic about basic needs. This is also your task in the discovery process. Ask questions that tell you what your customer needs. If you are selling automobiles, these would be questions like:

> "Is this vehicle for work or personal use?"
> "Do you need room for passengers?"
> "Do you plan on towing anything with this vehicle?"

Asking questions that help you understand how the vehicle will be used will enable you to be a blessing to your customer. Those questions allow you to match the solution your company has to your customer's specific circumstances. This information will also be invaluable when you get to step five; Linking Logic.

One of the most often quoted sections of the Bible comes from Matthew's account of the Sermon on the Mount. Jesus covers many topics in his sermon, including our proclivity to worry. Jesus asks, "Can any of you by worrying add a single moment to your life?" Notice that Jesus is not appealing to logic with this question. Rather, he is appealing to our emotions. It may be a logical argument, but Jesus is connecting that logic to a powerful emotion; worry. You also need to ask questions that tie to emotion, specifically, desires. To do this, ask questions that tell you what your customer wants. If you are selling homes, these would be questions like:

"Would you like to be able to see the lake from your master bedroom window?"

"Would you like to live in a neighborhood that includes membership in the Country Club?"

"Would living in a neighborhood with the highest rated schools in town be appealing to you?"

By asking questions that help you understand what your customer desires, you can exceed your customer's expectations. If you have a solution that is logical and also coincides with your customer's wish list, you are well on your way to moving the customer into the next stage of the process. Uncovering wants will play a critical role in step 6; Emotional Involvement.

At another point in Matthew's account of Jesus' life, two blind men pursue Jesus when He leaves a synagogue's leaders house and chase him down. They cry out for mercy, asking Jesus to give them their sight. Jesus asks them a simple question, "Do you believe that I am able to do this?" For many believers, fear that God can't actually do the things He claims He can do becomes very real. That fear can keep us from the perfectly planned life that God has prepared for each of us. In the same way, the fear that your customer is feeling about making a purchase from you is also very real and very powerful. To overcome that fear, you first need to identify it. To do that, ask questions that tell you about your customer's fears. If you are selling business software, these would be questions like:

"Are you personally responsible for the results of this software implementation?"

"Will this purchase have a significant impact on your annual budget?"

"Are the employees who will actually be using the software excited about the change?"

Remember, selling is the art of reducing a customer's fear of making a mistake. If you don't address the fear your customer has, it is very unlikely the transaction will occur. These questions will come into play in step 7; Close. If you fail to uncover and or address the fear your customer has, you will be fighting an uphill battle that you are not likely to win. Fear is a powerful deterrent. On the flip side, if you can root up and eradicate the fear your customer has, your customer is on their way to a solution to their problem and you are set to earn a nice commission.

Discovery is almost always the longest step in the selling process, regardless if you have a two month sales cycle or a one call close. Learn to ask great questions.

STEP FOUR: HOOK

There is nothing more powerful than being emotionally connected to a decision. Just in the last couple of weeks, my wife and I purchased a cruise to celebrate our 25th wedding anniversary. While we have been on several cruises in the past, we have never done an Alaskan cruise and we are very excited about the opportunity that God has given us to experience this trip.

I have several reasons to be excited about this trip. I was born near Seattle and lived in a small town not too far from there called Port Orchard until I was six years old. I was able to go back to "The Ranch" I grew up on one time when I was in High School. My visit lasted about 15 minutes. I was traveling to Alaska to go fishing with my dad, and having a three hour layover in Seattle, he grabbed us a cab to show me where I had lived. It is an amazing 20 acre piece of land overlooking the Puget Sound. It is so gorgeous in fact, that after it changed hands, one of the new owners turned it into a golf course. My Dad always called it "The Ranch" but we didn't have livestock. What we did have was trees. Lots and lots of trees. I still remember my older brothers cutting down trees to cut up for firewood, which they would sell out of the back of a pick-up for money when they were in high school. They would cut the small branches off and I would drag them away, and they would let me believe I was a big help in their firewood cutting business.

Just writing that paragraph is bringing back a flood of memories about my childhood. My wife and I have extended our trip to spend an extra day in Washington so that we can go look at my childhood home. I am so excited, I can't wait. I have a deep emotional attachment to this upcoming trip. Based on what I just told you, do you think I am more attached to the trip we just purchased or the money that we spent to purchase the trip?

Every product can have an emotional hook for your customer. When I was in the floor covering business, it was commonly the way a customer's home would look when they had their new floors installed. It is your job to connect the outcome to the customer. If you are selling new carpet, you might ask a question like "How would you feel if your guests came into this room and instead of this old worn out brown shag, they saw this beautiful beige saxony, making the room look so much bigger and brighter?" If you are selling sheds, you might ask "How would it feel to know that all of your keepsakes and lawn equipment are not only safe from the weather, but also out of your garage, so that you can protect your car, one of your most expensive assets, from the elements as well?"

Notice that these question are about feelings. Emotional involvement connects feelings and desires, not logic. That is another step. In this phase of the sales process, focus on how the product will impact them emotionally. If you have been asking a lot of questions, you should know what questions to ask to connect their emotions to the product. Remember, selling is the art of reducing the customer's fear of making a mistake. Many times the emotional hook is related to their fear. Let's say that you are selling investments. Let's also say that you have a customer that wants to invest money that will be used for her son's college education. During the process of "Discovery" you uncovered the fact that your customer is afraid she may make the wrong investment choice and that her son would not have all the money he needs to go to college. Once you have found the investment product that will best serve your customer, you might ask "How would it feel to be able to go to bed at night, knowing that your son will have every penny he needs to complete his education by the time he graduates from High School?" You are creating an emotional attachment to the product while reducing the customer's fear of making a mistake at the same time.

Want to see a demo? Visit www.JohnJKimmel.com

STEP FIVE: LINK LOGIC

In contrast to emotional involvement, linking logic in the sales process has nothing to do with how the customer feels. Linking logic is the process of transferring the knowledge that you already have forward to your customer. You have told them what they should buy and why, this is when you prove it.

When we first moved to Texas, my wife and I hired a real estate agent to find us a home. After months of looking and inspections, we excitedly took possession of our new home. My wife and I had become friends with our Realtor by then and we invited her over for coffee one afternoon. In the course of conversation about the Texas summer heat, she said "Make sure you water your foundation once it gets hot." I laughed and made a joke about the house growing if

I watered it, to which Jodi replied, "No, really, you need to water your foundation to keep it from cracking." I smiled, and told her thank you for her advice. You see, having spent my entire life around house and building foundations and floors, I was very confident that I knew everything there was to know, and was certain that it was not necessary to water my foundation.

The next day at the office, I told a buddy of mine the story about watering my foundation, knowing full well that he would think it was funny. My friend listened to my story and then said, "She is right you know, you do have to water your foundation here in North Texas." I laughed until I noticed that he was not laughing. "Come on, I am not that gullible!" I said. My friend just looked at me and said, "On your way home, stop at Lowes. They have foundation hoses on sale this week."

As it turns out, there is so much clay in the ground where I live, that if you don't keep the dirt around your slab moist in the summer, it will cause your foundation to crack. My realtor was right.

I tell you that story because at this very moment I am in the process of shopping for a contractor to do a foundation repair on my house. The last couple years I was lax in replacing worn out, sun cracked foundation hoses and now the foundation of my house is cracking like the hull of the titanic, breaking stone floors and opening gaps in the sheet rock. I am still getting estimates, but it looks like I am going to have to spend about $20,000 to fix my home, an expense I have a serious aversion to.

Here is where linking logic comes into play. I already have emotional involvement in the decision to fix my foundation. I feel it every time I look at a broken tile or cracked gout line. What the salesperson who gets my order to repair my house needs to do now is justify the expense of repairs.

The truth is that if I choose not to fix my foundation, the problem will only get worse. As the problem gets worse, so will the amount of damage I need to repair after the foundation is fixed.

A good presentation on this does not need to be fancy or complicated. Something like "Mr. Kimmel, you can choose to spend $20,000 now and fix your foundation. My company will do a quality job and we guarantee our work. Once we are done, you will need to make some repairs to your home, which will cost you a little bit more. You could also choose to continue waiting on your foundation repair, like you have been doing. At some point you will be forced to make the repair and by then it will cost a lot more. You will also have more damage to your house, maybe even your roof by then, which could get very expensive in a hurry. Which course of action do you think makes the most sense?"

Linking logic is simple. Connect the customer's mind with their heart regarding the purchase. If you can do that, you are ready to close the sale. Remember, selling is the art of reducing a customer's fear of making a mistake. Linking logic usually revolves around fear and your ability to reduce it.

STEP SIX: CLOSE

At this point in the process, you have done your prospecting, introduced yourself, discovered your customer's needs and fears and tied them emotionally and logically to your product or service. If you have done all that flawlessly, then at this point you can call yourself a master conversationalist. If you want to call yourself a salesperson, however, then you must take this next step and close the sale.

Larry loved houses and real estate. So much so that he left a career in outside building material sales and got his real estate agents license. Everyone loved to have Larry around as he really is a nice guy, so he quickly gathered a small clientele of potential home buyers. After a few months, Larry asked me to lunch. I had no idea the conversation would end up as a sales training session, but we met at a burger joint and that's what happened. In between bites of greasy, cheesy burgers Larry confided in me that he was really getting frustrated with being a real estate agent. When I asked him why, Larry said "Half my customers want to see every single house on the planet and don't buy anything, and the other half use me to find what they want and then buy it from another agent." "Do you have them sign an agreement before you start viewing properties?" I asked. "Oh, yah, they all have to sign the agreement that they will use me for the transaction, but what am I going to do? Sue them? That's not my style, plus I probably wouldn't get anything out of it but bad publicity." At that, I started to ask him a series of questions. After a conversation that had gone on long enough that I was down to my last two French fries, I asked Larry, "Are you asking your customers to buy the house you are showing them?" "John, buying a house isn't like that. It's not like I am selling them a toaster. People need to see a bunch of houses before they see the right one. You can't just ask them to buy every house you show them." Larry countered. "Is there something wrong with the houses you are showing your customers?" I asked. Larry responded, "No, of course not. In fact, our company's inventory alone includes some really nice places." "Are they overpriced?" I asked. Larry said "No, you can't really get away with that in this market." Next I asked, "Are you showing people houses that meet their requirements? You know, this many bedrooms, this many baths, etc.?" Larry said, "Well sure. People would get frustrated with me pretty quickly if I didn't take them to houses that were the type they wanted to see." "Okay, let me get this straight." I said. "You are taking your customers to see houses that meet all of their needs, are in good condition and are well priced, but you don't think you should ask them to buy the house they are looking at. Is that correct?" Larry sidestepped my question and said, "Well, you can't just ask your customer to buy the first house they look at." I replied "I'm not sure I am onboard with that, but let's say you are correct. How many houses do they need to see? Two? Ten? Fifty?" Larry said, "It could be different for everyone. Maybe someone would by the first house but then someone else might want to see twenty." I asked Larry "How do you know that the person you are showing a house to isn't the one that will buy the house you are standing in? If you ask them to put an offer on the house you are showing, but they want to see others just to make sure, can't they just tell you that when you ask them to buy the house?"

That month, Larry started selling homes.

STEP SEVEN: FOLLOW UP

It is 6:30 pm on a Friday night. Susan and Carl are on their way to dinner to celebrate her big sale that day. Carl listens intently as Susan recants everything that transpired earlier with her customer. She is excited to tell Carl how she masterfully got past all of the customer's anti-salesperson walls to discover their true needs. Susan knew that the product her customers wanted to buy was truly going to make a difference in their lives and her enthusiasm showed. She almost couldn't wait for the product to arrive so that her customers could start using it right away. In fact she had put the product on hold with the manufacturer half way through the sales process, just in case they decided to move forward. That way, once the customer decided to buy, they would make the shipping deadline for the day and have it by Monday. Suddenly Susan stops speaking and a look of dread crosses her face. Carl asks, "What's the matter?" Susan is clearly disturbed. "I forgot to place the order!" Susan exclaims. "I put it on hold but I never called back to place the order! Now they will not get it on Monday like I promised!"

Have you ever been there? Can you relate to Susan? There is nothing worse than doing every part of your job flawlessly and then disappointing your customer with poor follow up. Failing to do your job after the sale will cause you to get cancellations, inhibit future purchases from your existing customers and make it nearly impossible to get referrals.

Every organization is different. Some salespeople are responsible for many logistical follow up procedures and some have very few. The first thing you need to do is identify what your actual responsibilities are. Perhaps you are responsible for entering invoices or placing orders or scheduling delivery, etc. Make an actual written list of every single item you need to accomplish, no matter how small. By the way, if you really want to impress your boss, once you think the list is complete, approach him or her and say "I really want to be great at follow up, so I made a list of everything I need to do after I make a sale. Would you please take a moment to review my list and let me know if I forgot anything?" Personally, I have never had a single salesperson ask me that question, but would be ecstatic if one did.

The next step is to actually use the list. For some of you who are less technologically advanced, it could be as simple as having a copy of your list for every customer and crossing out the follow up items as you complete them. For others it might mean incorporating tasks into Microsoft Outlook or setting up fields in your CRM. Whatever it looks like for you, do it. It will put you into a class by yourself. Remember, your customers remember the last contact with you more vividly than their first contact, so make sure the last thing they experience is great follow up.

STEP EIGHT: REFERRALS

Joe Girard is widely regarded as the greatest car salesman who ever lived. What is most interesting to me is that while I am sure he was adept in all of the sales stages, his incredible success truly can be attributed to what he accomplished after the initial sale.

Joe sold 13,001 cars in just fifteen years. Assuming five day work weeks and fifty weeks on the job per year, that is nearly three and one half cars per day. If you have ever sold cars before, you know just how incredible that is. Even more incredible is that most of those sales came from repeat customers and referrals. Joe had a wise practice that seems so simple, yet very few of us have followed in his footsteps and copied him. Joe would send a simple card to everyone who purchased a vehicle from him. It was always different in size, color or shape, so as not to look like junk mail and it always contained the same simple message. If the card was being mailed in July, the card would say, "I like you, Happy 4th of July. Joe Girard" If it was November the card would say, "I like you, Happy Thanksgiving. Joe Girard" If it was February, the card would say, "I like you, Happy President's Day. Joe Girard"

Every month he would stay in front of his customers with a simple card, and it made him the number one car and truck salesman in the United States, twelve years in a row. People enjoyed buying cars from Joe Girard. They wanted to buy cars from him and would actually look forward to their next purchase and would regularly tell others about

Joe. Do your customers enjoy buying from you? If they do, are you asking them for referrals?

Imagine that a new restaurant opened up in the town that you live in. You have been wanting to try it because it serves the type of dishes you really enjoy. After you are seated, a happy, helpful waitress takes your order. Your food arrives quickly and smells amazing. You are thrilled to discover that it tastes even better than it smells. All through the meal, your waitress serves you impeccably. During the meal the owner drops by your table, thanks you for coming and makes sure that you are happy with your meal. When the check comes, you're reminded of the great value this meal has been, considering the quality and service you have received. As you happily head for the exit, you encounter the owner again. He shakes your hand and confirms that you enjoyed your meal and received superior service. Upon confirming that you did truly enjoy it and will definitely come back, the owner asks you a simple question, "Since we have just opened, and many people don't know about our restaurant yet, would you mind telling some friends that you enjoyed your meal here today?"

What would you say? You would likely say "Of course I will! In fact, I already texted a buddy of mine back at the office, telling him that I found a new restaurant that we are going to eat at the next time it is my turn to choose!"

Many salespeople are afraid to ask for referrals because they are afraid the customer will say no or that the question will somehow be awkward. The question will only be awkward if you have not done a good job or kept the customer's best interest in mind during the sale. People are inclined to help people that have helped them and they like.

So how and when do you ask for a referral? If you sell inside a one call close model, the time to ask for a referral is at the end of the transaction, while they are still with you face to face or on the phone. You don't need to be fancy or complicated. After the transaction is complete, simply say something like, "Thank you for partnering with us on XYZ software, do you know anyone else, who, like you, would benefit from this system?" In most cases, when presented conversationally, people will answer that they do know someone. Let's say your customer refers you to Joe Smith. "Would you be willing to share Joe's contact information with me?" is the next question to ask, followed by "Could you call Joe and let him know that I will be calling?"

If your customer grabs her phone and starts making the call, let them do it! While they are dialing, add, "Thank you for calling them now, would you mind introducing me to them after you tell them why you are calling?" When your customer hands you the phone, be professional and to the point. "Hello Joe, I am here with your friend, Holly. She just took advantage of something that she thinks would be very helpful for you as well. Is there a good time for us to have a quick conversation to see if this would make sense for you?" Get the appointment and get off the phone. Make sure you thank your customer for the referral.

If your customer gives you Joe's contact info, but does not initiate the call, that's ok. Simply say "Thank you for giving me the opportunity to talk to Joe. If you could call him this afternoon, I will make sure I reach out to him before the end of the day. Would that be alright? It's absolutely imperative that you call the referral when you say that you will call. You also want to keep your customer in the loop regarding the person they referred you to. For example, you might call your customer that evening and say "Good evening Holly, I am calling to make sure you love your new software. I also want to let you know that I talked to Joe, and he is going to come by the office this Tuesday." In a world where contact information is abused terribly, it is important to confirm to your customer that you are a professional, and following up on their referral appropriately is one of the best ways to do that.

If you are not a one stop transaction, the best time to ask for a referral is when the transaction is completed. For example, if you sell appliances and you are going to install a washer and dryer at Bob and Mary's house this Thursday, then the best time to ask for a referral is right at the conclusion of the installation. A possible exception would be if perhaps your company was having a sale that ended before that time, or there was some other compelling reason to get the referral before the completion of the job.

Do you know which customers are most likely to give you a referral? The customer that already gave you a referral. Many salespeople make the mistake of getting a referral and then never asking the same customer for another one. Whether the referred person purchases from you or not, make sure you follow up with your original customer to thank them for the opportunity to help their friend. This is a great time to ask for the next referral. Do you have a set follow up schedule? Do you call after a week, a month or a year to make sure everything is going perfectly? These are great times to ask for referrals. They are also a great time to get upgrades, and new sales. Following up is so simple and so powerful, but almost no one does it. Being great at follow up will set you apart from your competition and it will also be a light to unbelievers. When you act differently than the rest of the World, you will draw people to you and have more opportunities to sell Christ, which is far more valuable than anything else we could ever persuade people to buy.

CHAPTER 11
MISSION
ACCOMPLISHED

EVERY SOLDIER WHO enters combat knows exactly what his mission is. Do you?

When I was a little boy in grade school, we were taught to fear two things: Global cooling (No, really, "Environmental experts" told us we were on the verge of the next ice age) and the impending nuclear attack from the Soviet Union. We did drills in school and watched movies featuring mushroom clouds and most of us had to wake our parents at one time or another because of the nightmares those movies inspired. The Cold War was very real to us who lived through it because the threat was real. The US and USSR had enough nuclear firepower to destroy the Earth and we are afraid that the Soviets would use it.

In 1980 we elected a new President and in January of 1981 Ronald Reagan took office. Less than eleven years later, on Christmas day, 1991, the Soviet hammer and sickle flag lowered for the last time over the Kremlin, Mikhail Gorbachev resigned his post as president of the Soviet Union, and the Cold War was officially over. Reagan's legacy is highlighted by his handling of the war, but it really boiled down to having a great plan.

President Reagan and his advisors had devised a plan that would include economic, political, military, ideological, and moral components, and they carried it out. It was not an accident that we won the war. The United States had a plan and knew exactly what they wanted to achieve. Selling is no different.

Just like a military plan, before you make a call or talk to a customer it is imperative that you know exactly where you want the conversation to end. You need to ask yourself a series of questions that include: "What is my purpose for this sales call?" "What specific things do I want to accomplish on this call?" And "How am I going to get there?"

Before you blurt out an answer to the first question, "What is the purpose of my sales call?" I want you to stop and think about it. While for some of us selling inexpensive simple items, the purpose of every call may be to make a sale, for most of us selling in more complex systems, this is not always the case. The purpose of your call may be to get an appointment to make a presentation. You might need to get a specific piece of information having to do with logistics or requirements. Not every sales call is supposed to end with a sale, but more of yours will end that way if you consciously think about what your purpose is on every call before you make it.

Next, I want you to write down what specific things you need to accomplish on your call. If you sell homes, your list might include things like "Find out how many bedrooms the client wants." or "Ask how big a yard he needs." and

"Are schools in the neighborhood important?" If you sell computer systems to large corporations, your list might include things like "Find out which departments will be using the system" and "Find out why they want to replace the system they have." Or "Determine who is stalling the implementation." Regardless of what you sell, there is information you will need to be able to help your customer and close the sale.

Once you have basic information, you need to get to your customers pain. What are they experiencing that is causing them to talk to you. Many times, you will find clues to your customer's pain in their answers they gave you earlier and you need to have questions ready to dig deeper. For example, if your client tells you they are looking for a home that has "Great schools," that might be a potential pain point. You might say something like this; "You mentioned that you wanted great schools, have you lived somewhere that did not have great schools?" and listen for their answer. Listen for attitude and tone of voice. If you are face to face, watch their body language. If they reply "Yes, we thought we were moving right next to a great school when we purchased our current home, but we found out otherwise once our daughter started attending."

Be prepared to dig even deeper. A follow up question might look like; "I am hearing that your new home being in a place with a great school is very important to you. Would you say that this is number one on your list of requirements to finding your new home? If the customer says "No," then keep asking questions, but if they say "Yes," then you have found a pain point. You also now know one of the things they are afraid of. Remember, selling is the art of reducing a customer's fear of making a mistake. Once you find the perfect home with the perfect schools, that customer will not buy it until you have reduced their fear of buying a house that does not have great schools.

For every sales call there is a mission. Create a map of where you are, where you want to go and the questions you need to ask in order to get to your destination.

CHAPTER 12
MAKE A NEW PLAN, STAN

ONE OF THE biggest challenges that salespeople have is effective use of their time. The vast majority of us are non-linear thinkers, which means we have the ability to alter the course of our thoughts at the drop of a hat. While this makes us agile and effective in the sales process, it also means we have a propensity to plan our time use poorly. Even when we do make a plan, we often find ourselves off course and struggling to get all of our tasks completed before the sun goes down. If you ever hear yourself telling your boss something like "I intended to do that this morning, but Mrs. Jones called and I had to go drop her off a sample for that big job. Then the phone rang and I had a chance to bid a new project…" then you know what I mean. We know that some things are more important than others, but our plans fail because we fail to have a real plan.

If you want your plan to be successful, you need to work backwards. Start with your long term goals and then start determining the steps to get there. Begin by deciding where you want to be in one year. From there, identify what you would need to have accomplished on a quarterly basis to reach those goals. Next, break your quarterly goals down into monthly goals and then the month into weekly steps. Once you have your goals dissected into smaller pieces, your mind can work on how to accomplish them in a much more efficient manner. Let's say you sell couches and have a sales goal to sell one hundred couches this year. It is easy to get overwhelmed by large goals, and your mind may struggle with how you can accomplish that goal, so break it down. One hundred couches in a year is twenty five couches in a quarter. Twenty five couches in a quarter is a little over eight couches per month, which is about two couches per week.

Now that you have your goal broken down into weeks, your next step is to determine what you need to do this week to sell two couches. What actions do you need to take? How many sales calls do you need to make? What roadblocks do you need to clear? Whose help or buy in do you need? Once you have those things written down, break your week down into days and focus on those things that you have determined are critical for your success first, before you add anything else to your daily plans.

The next thing you need to do is learn your ABC's. Most sales people have some control of what customers they see, when, and how often. If you are in this position then it is critical that you segregate your customers into A, B and C categories. There is no rocket science here. An A customer is a customer that can or is producing a lot of revenue, a B customer is in the middle and a C customer is only capable of a small return or is a longshot. While categorizing your customers can be done with many formats and levels of complexity, the point is this: Spend more time on those customers that can bring you the greatest return and very little time on those that will not bring you a return.

It would not be unusual to have twenty percent of your pipeline filled with "A" customers, sixty percent with "B's," and twenty percent with "C's." It would also not be unusual if your best use of time meant you would spend fifty percent of your time on your A customers (Even though it is only twenty percent of your pipeline), forty percent of your time on your B customers (Although it is sixty percent of your total customers), and ten percent of your time on your C customers (The last twenty percent of your pipeline). In this way you are focusing your time where it will have the greatest return for you and your employer.

Some of you who are in retail, for example, do not get to choose which customer you see next, but even you can control how effectively you use your time. If you have a customer that has great potential to be a large sale, then spend extra time on that customer. If you have someone that is a small transaction, then be professional and give them the care they deserve, but do not spend extra time chit-chatting with them. Move on to your next prospect and use your time wisely.

The last thing you need to do is compartmentalize your time to be most effective. If your day consists of prospecting, making sales calls and filing paperwork, then do each of those things in blocks. Start your day by doing all of your prospecting work. Once you are finished, then make all of your calls. Last, finish your day by doing all of your paperwork. Instead of doing what most sales people do, which is research, call, do paperwork and then repeat this over and over, you will discover that by focusing on one activity at a time, you are able to do all three more quickly and efficiently, allowing you to make extra sales calls and be more profitable.

Solomon said, "Go to the ant, you sluggard; consider its ways and be wise! It has no commander, no overseer or ruler, yet it stores its provisions in summer and gathers its food at harvest." A lack of planning equals a poor future, but a well thought out plan will bring success to your family.

CHAPTER 13
WHOSE IMAGE DO YOU
SEE IN THE MIRROR?

SELF-IMAGE IS CRITICAL to success in selling. Are you seeing Jesus when you look in the mirror?

Like many competitive people, I often need to remind myself of the Apostle Paul's words, "For through the grace given to me I say to everyone among you not to think more highly of himself than he ought to think; but to think so as to have sound judgment, as God has allotted to each a measure of faith." God knew that we would struggle with pride. He knew it would be easy for us to fool ourselves into thinking that the many blessings he would lavish on us are somehow the result of our own accomplishments, even though Christ's half-brother James told us, "Every good thing given and every perfect gift is from above, coming down from the Father of lights, with whom there is no variation or shifting shadow."

So now that we have a biblical perspective on who we are not, let's focus on who the Bible says we are. While we were all born in sin and were powerless to overcome our own wickedness, God tells us in His word that "Therefore if anyone is in Christ, *he is* a new creature; the old things passed away; behold, new things have come." The Word goes on to refer to us as every one of the following:

- Complete
- Born Again
- Victorious
- Forgiven
- Royalty
- Free Rom
- God's workmanship
- Alive
- Fearless
- Untouchable by evil
- Holy
- Blameless
- Possessing the mind of Christ
- Possessing peace
- Righteous
- Wise
- Powerful
- Lacking nothing
- Able to do all things
- Heir to the Kingdom of God
- More than conquerors
- Overcomers
- Showing His divine nature
- Ambassadors
- Chosen
- Priests
- The Temple of God
- Elected

- Merciful
- Kind rom
- Humble
- Redeemed
- Delivered
- Called
- Strengthened
- Loved

The Characteristics above embody the very nature of Christ Himself. Each of those descriptions is more than we could hope for, or deserve, without God. That is why the sacrifice Jesus made on the cross is so important to us. Jesus embodies everything that is good and perfect while we are wretched and broken, deserving to die for our sins. Without the cross, God would look down on us and see who we are, but now Jesus has given himself as a replacement to receive our punishment. Jesus went on to invite us into a relationship with him that is divine in nature, making us one body with Christ. Jesus is the head of that body and our intercessor. Because of this amazing relationship we now share with Christ, when God the Father looks down from Heaven at us, He does not see us as we were, broken and in sin. God sees us as we are now; Holy and blameless. When God looks at us now, He sees his Son.

Who do you see when you look in the mirror? Do you see Jesus? Do you see a man or woman living in the Power of God Almighty or do you see someone flawed and feeble? If you have given your life to Christ, but do not see yourself as everything on the list above, then it is time for a change of perspective. The people we were before Christ cannot do anything good for themselves, their families or their customers, but Royal Ambassadors to the King of Kings can have tremendous impact for the good of others.

I realize that some of you reading this do not have a relationship with Christ yet. If you find yourself in this place, I want you to know that every good thing I am claiming above can be yours. Peace, freedom, forgiveness, and power can all be words to describe the person you can become. You cannot buy those things and neither can you earn them. They are only available as the free gift we call salvation. I will discuss this further at the end of the book.

CHAPTER 14
READY, SET, GO!

MANY PEOPLE BELIEVED that their lives should be compartmentalized. They think that work is separate from family is separate from church. That is simply not true. Your life is your life and you should be the same man or woman at home as you are at work. The same in a crowd as you are alone. The same on Sunday as you are on Wednesday. Don't be deceived into thinking that a chapter dedicated entirely to faith is out of place in a sales book. It may be the most important chapter of all.

By now you are likely seeing another pattern in these pages; if you want to be a successful salesperson, life is not about you, it is about others. Recently, a pastor at Lake Pointe Church where I teach, did a sermon about joy. He used a great acronym that fits perfect in our conversation. The Acronym was:

J – Jesus First
O – Others Second
Y – You Will Experience Joy

When it comes to sales, there is a similar principle that looks like this:

J – Jesus First
O – Others Second
Y – You Will Experience Success in Sales

JESUS FIRST

Putting Jesus first is not just rhetoric. There are real, tangible things that need to happen in your life to make this a reality. Each of the items listed below is important to your spiritual health and none can be ignored. When you do all of these things together, you will find that they don't just add to your spiritual life, they multiply it. Have you ever wondered why some people are so much more faithful and fired up about Christ than others? Usually, those folks have figured this out and are doing the things we are about to talk about. They are living lives of purpose, meaning and joy, and they inspire us to do the same.

STUDY

Sylvia showed up to class ready for a conflict. She had looked at the topic for the weekend's bible study class and noticed that it was on the sanctity of life. Sylvia had always identified herself as a pro-choice Christian and her position had caused conflict with other Believers before. As the teacher of the class, I try to greet people as they come into the room. That day it was clear that something was wrong with Sylvia. She and I had recently had some doctrinal disagreements and one of them had been a deeply emotional issue for Sylvia. Being more sensitive to her mood than usual, it was clear that this might be a difficult hour.

I got the class started and dug into the lesson. Abortion is always a sensitive topic to teach on because it has affected so many families. Many times women who have had abortions in the past only to later realize how they had been deceived on the subject live with unreleased guilt. That turned out to be the case on this day. Toward the end of my lesson, one of the ladies asked to share something with the class. She opened up and told us that she had two abortions and how those deaths had weighed so heavily upon her for so many years.

I was encouraged greatly by the response of the class as they loved on this woman. It was a textbook example of "Hate the sin and love the sinner." As this dramatic moment unfolded I saw a hand go into the air. It was Sylvia. I have to admit that I cringed inside. I thought "Oh, no, Sylvia is going to going to say something that could undo what is happening in the class right now." As I was justifying my actions to myself, that still, small voice spoke to me. The Holy Spirit was telling me to call on Sylvia. I mentally sparred with the Spirit briefly, praying, "God, are you sure? This is an amazing moment we are having here. Sylvia could completely change the mood in the class if I let her talk." The Holy Spirit responded clearly, "Let her speak." I obeyed. "Sylvia, did you have something to add?" I prepared myself for what was to come next.

"I have been pro-choice my entire life and I came here tonight prepared to tell you why you were wrong." Sylvia said as I braced myself. "But I had never heard the verses that we studied tonight. I never knew how God really felt about abortion. Now I know that God is clearly against abortion. I was wrong. I came here pro-choice, but I am going home pro-life." That day was one of the most rewarding, encouraging days of my life. Sometimes just when we think that our ministry isn't bearing fruit, God will surprise us with a spiritual victory.

I tell that story because it is such a clear illustration of why we need to study God's word. Other people that claimed they were Christians had told Sylvia that abortion was not a sin and she believed them. She never looked into the Word herself to verify that what those people said was actually true. No one can study the Bible for you. Not even your pastor. You need to make time to study for yourself and discover who God truly is, as He reveals Himself through his Holy Word.

Not too many years ago I would have strongly suggested you go out and buy a good study Bible, a concordance, a bible dictionary and even a few different translations of the bible like the NIV, NKJV, NASB and even the Living Bible as references to help you study scripture. By the way, the Living Bible should not be your primary source for study as it adds text for clarification purposes. NASB and NIV are my favorite translations to use on a daily basis, because of their easy to understand language and accuracy to the original text.

While I still recommend that you get all of those things and have them handy during your study time, I am happy to tell you that all of those things are now available online for free, so if you have internet access, there is no reason not to have those resources at your fingertips. There are also tremendous free resources available to supplement your study on every book of the Bible and most of the topics you can think of.

When Timothy was pastoring the church in Ephesus, Paul sent him what would be his final letter of encouragement. Paul said, "Do your best to present yourself to God as one approved, a worker who does not need to be ashamed and who correctly handles the word of truth." Paul knew that in order for Timothy to be effective, he had to have a keen grasp of the Word of God. In fact, the implications here are that Timothy needed to know it so well that he would be able to teach it to others. This holds true for us as well. You and I cannot put Jesus first if we don't know what He wants from us. Timothy, Paul and those of their time had to rely on a few written copies of God's word, the occasional letter and to a large degree, oral practice of the Word. Said another way, they mostly had to talk to one another to stay rooted in the Word of God.

We have an enormous advantage that they did not enjoy. We have millions of copies of the bible. We have uncountable books and commentaries to make sure we understand what the Bible is telling us and with the internet, it is all but a click away, if we choose to seek guidance. More than any other generation before us, we have no excuse for failing to study God's word. Regardless of which translation of the Bible you choose, there is one thing that I know; God will honor your commitment to draw close to him and the Holy Spirit will enable you to understand what you seek to learn.

PRAYER

June of 2006 is a month I will never forget. My son was 10 years old and he was on his way to church camp. What made this camp special for us was that this year, as well as the previous year, I was going to camp with him, as a parent volunteer.

Wagon Train is a special place. Deep in the foothills of central California lies Kings Canyon National Forest and Hume Lake. Its snow fed crystal blue water is the setting for one of the most beautiful camps in the nation. The camp is divided into sections by age, and the area for nine and ten year olds is called Wagon Train. It is aptly named because the cabins are exactly that; covered wagons. Imagine a camp, entirely set on a hill. Fifty oversize wagons populate the top of the hill. Each one is big enough to hold a dozen bunk beds and the standard arrangement is a ten boys to one dad in the boy's side of the hill and the same ratio of girls to moms on the girl's side of the hill. As you come down the hill there are great facilities for the kids to worship as well as the bathrooms and showers that the parents can't wait to use each morning. Continuing down the hill is the mess hall, and trust me, after 200 kids eat a meal, there is always a mess. On a little further to the bottom of the hill is the parking area for those who chose to drive their own vehicles, instead of coming by bus.

On the morning of June 11, I set sail in my Dodge Caravan mini-van heading for Hume Lake. It is about a four hour drive from where we lived at the time and I had a half dozen 9 and 10 year olds from our church filling the other seats of the van. Our trip took a little longer than it should have that morning because I had a bad habit at the time. I had a two pack a day smoking habit that was almost three decades old and it had a terrible grip on me. Since I had kids in the car, I had to make several stops to smoke, so I would pull off the highway, stand outside the car in some parking lot and smoke as fast as I could to get my nicotine fix, then pull away, thinking of my next smoke stop.

The summer before had been a smoker's nightmare. Wagon Train keeps the kids (And parents) extremely busy from about six in the morning until ten at night. There are only a few times per day when the kids are in groups or at meals, that a smoker can slip away, run all the way down the hill to his car and smoke. Of course, there is no smoking anywhere in the camp, so my van was the closest place to go. I would smoke like crazy for a few minutes, getting as much nicotine as I possibly could, and then run back to where the kids were before I was needed again. I find it funny that somehow I thought I was the only one who knew what I was doing. The reality, of course, was that everyone in camp, from parent to child, knew what I was doing.

I had decided that 2006 was going to be different. I decided to couple the lack of access to cigarettes with smoking cessation aids and use Wagon Train to finally quit smoking. I went to the store and stocked up on the quit-smoking patch as well as the gum. I was a serious addict, so I believed I needed both. I also told my wife, my kids and my pastor what I was doing. I asked them to pray for me because I did not want to live this life anymore. I wanted to be free from the cigarettes for me and for my family.

So here I was, in the minivan, about to enter the gates of the camp. I pulled off the road and got out. I took out a cigarette and lit it. I stood there for a while, enjoying what I hoped was the last cigarette I would ever smoke. As I neared the end of my smoke, I prayed to God. I don't remember the exact words I prayed, but I know the gist of them. "Jesus, I need help. I can't do this alone. Please help me, I don't want to be this man anymore. Please." At that I dropped that cigarette into the dirt, crushed it out with my foot and got back into the van, entering the gates of the non-smoking camp.

Many of the parents volunteering were returning from the year before and I was happy to be reacquainted with some of the folks I had met in 2005. Then something awesome happened. Normally, there are ten kids and one parent per wagon, but somehow we had one extra parent and he was assigned to my cabin! This would be a game changer, I thought. He and I could give each other breaks and even take a shower without having to watch a pack of nine year olds. I also told Rob, my co-leader, about my plan to quit smoking. I was going to wear the nicotine patch 24 hours a day (The ones I was using were designed to be time released over a 24 hour period) and then supplement with the gum, as needed. Rob told me that he remembered how I would run down to my minivan every chance I got last year, and told me he would pray for me. I told him that I really appreciated that, especially since I had the patch on and was already wearing out a piece of the gum.

That day continued as expected – busy. By the time we finally drug ourselves into our cabin for the night, Rob asked me how the smoking struggle was going. I told him that I was doing ok. I was tentatively optimistic. He then asked me if it would be alright if he got up to shower at 5:00 am, which was a full hour early. He explained that a hot shower was on his short list of blessings in life, and wondered if he would mind if he snuck off each morning to indulge himself. I told him that I would be happy to watch the kids from five to six, especially since they would be asleep.

Day two started off as planned. Rob got his early shower and the whirlwind of activity was in full swing. One of my personal weaknesses is that I almost never read directions. As it turns out, nicotine gum actually has to be used in a certain way. The idea is simple…if you read the package. You are supposed to store the gum between your lip and gum and you only chew it when you are having cravings, as chewing the gum causes the release of the nicotine into your system. Since I never imagined that gum came with directions, I had been chewing away all day and by the afternoon, I had actually made myself sick to my stomach. Apparently, you can get too much nicotine. Who knew? Rob asked me why I was looking pale and after reading the box and discovering my mistake, I decided to stick with the patch and get rid of the gum. The ironic thing was, I had not actually had cravings, and I just enjoyed the rush that the chemical gave me.

Day three started much the way day two did. Rob took his early shower and then I got one while he wrangled the kids into the stalls to engage in the much needed dirt removal process. Worship and activities filled the day and the next thing we know it was mid-afternoon. Because Rob and I were sweating profusely trying to chase kids all over a soccer field, we stopped in the field together to laugh about how out of shape we had both become. Rob then asked me how the non-smoking was going. I told him that surprisingly, I felt great. No cravings at all. Then, suddenly, it dawned on me, I had never put on a new nicotine patch that morning. Rob could tell by the look on my face that something was up. "What's wrong?" he asked. As I pulled up the sleeve of my t-shirt, I pulled off the patch and answered "I forgot to put on a new patch this morning. I haven't had any nicotine in at least eight hours." "Do you need to go get a new one" Rob asked. "No." I replied. "If I have gone this long, I think I will wait. I actually feel great. I am shocked, but I am not craving a cigarette at all." That elicited a big smile from Rob who suggested we get back to chasing children, which we did.

Days four, five and six were more of the same. Rob would always rise first. We would use the tag team method to watch the kids all day, and inevitably he would ask how I was doing with the smoking. My answer was always the same; I was doing great. Somehow, I was not craving a cigarette. I was baffled. I should explain that my addiction was severe. I started sneaking cigarettes when I was seven years old. I always looked older than I really was and many small stores were loose about selling smokes in those days. Consequently, I had a two pack a day habit that was in full swing by the time I was 12. For me, smoking was part of living, I couldn't even remember a time that smoking had not been part of my life. But somehow, that was changing, and it was good.

Day seven was departure day, but for me it started extra early. Sound asleep and snug in my sleeping bag, I was jostled awake by someone shaking me. I opened my groggy eyes to see Rob standing over me. "John," He whispered, "Wake up." I looked around and replied "What happened. Is everything ok?" while I tried to shake the cobwebs from my mind. Rob said, "Everything is fine, but I need you to get up. It's important." I'm not sure if I complied because I wanted to or if I was just too tired to argue, but a minute later, I found myself in the dark, breathing in the crisp morning mountain air. I followed Rob down the hill and was surprised when we kept going past the showers. Somehow, in my own mind, I assumed there was some sort of bathroom emergency, like a broken shower or toilet that he needed help with, but we kept walking. We walked all the way to the mess hall at the bottom of the hill. Rob opened the door, and holding it open said "After you." I walked past him into the open dining room. There were 21 total parent volunteers that year, and I found myself in the room with the other 19. All of them looked at me and greeted me good morning. I was completely confused. Clearly they were expecting me, but my tired mind was struggling to figure out why.

Rob walked up behind me, and putting his hand on my shoulder said, "John, can you please tell the group about how it's been going with you trying to quit smoking?" "Huh?" was all I could manage. Rob repeated his request for me to tell them how it was going with smoking and if I could share some of the details of the last week with them. I was still completely dumbfounded, but obliged, telling them about the last week and how amazed I was that I had not had any nicotine for several days now and yet was experiencing no cravings at all. As I told them the story, I noticed many of the other counselors smiling and some were even crying. It was obvious to Rob that I was still trying to figure out what was going on, so as I finished my story, Rob said, "John, you know, it doesn't actually take me a full hour to take a shower in the morning." This did not make things any clearer for me, and whatever look I had on my face must have displayed that fact because Rob responded by laughing out loud. Rob continued "John, every morning when I left the cabin at 5:00 am, I did not go straight to the shower. Every morning I would get up and come here. Actually, John, all of us (he swept his hand across the room pointing to the other parent volunteers) have been meeting here from five to five thirty, so that we could pray for you."

I was starting to understand. "Rob," I asked, "Are you saying that all of you have been meeting here every morning just to pray for me to quit smoking?" Rob said, "That's right. That's why I wanted to bring you down here so everyone could hear how God has responded to our prayers." Now I was the one who was crying. My knees were weak. I have seen people return from this camp looking like they have spent a week at Shawshank. This camp, while rewarding and powerful, is also exhausting, and all of these Christian brothers and sisters had added to their burden, getting up an hour early, every single day, just to pray for me. I was without words. All I could do was say "Thank you, thank you." As I cried. There were people all around me. They were hugging me and crying with me and all of us knew that something very special had happened there that week. We all got to experience the power of prayer and we all got to share in the miracle that God so generously bestowed on me.

As I write this, it has been ten years, one month and twenty three days since I snuffed out that last cigarette while parked outside the gate of Hume Lake Christian Camp's

Wagon Train. Not only have I never smoked another cigarette, I have never even had another craving to do so.

Do not ever underestimate the power of prayer. There
is no amount of training, no course you can take, no skills
you can learn, and no techniques you can practice that will
make you a successful salesperson apart from God.

If you want to have a powerful career, you will find
it in Him, not in yourself. Prayer is the means we use to
communicate with God. He wants us to talk to Him. He
also wants us to enlist those brothers and sisters around us
to pray as well. If you are married, have children, are a
part of a small group at church, you must be asking those
believers to pray for you as well.

QUIET TIME

Bobby and his father Robert were having a conversation one
day. As usual, Robert was only half listening to his son while
he tapped away on the keyboard of his laptop. Frustrated
with his father's lack of attention, Bobby confronted him
with a riddle. Bobby said, "Dad, you're the driver of a bus.
There are nineteen men, five women and two children on
board. At the first stop, seven men get off and two women
get on. At the next stop, five men get off, but no one gets on.
At the third stop, one woman gets off with her child and two
men get on. So here is the question: What is the name of
the bus driver?" Rolling his eyes, Robert says, "How should
I know?" "See Dad, I told you that you never listen! At the
beginning I said, '*You* are the driver of a bus.'"

If you are anything like me, you like to talk. Because of
the way I am wired to always have my mouth running, one
of the hardest skills for me to develop has been the art of
listening. Regardless of whether you are talking with a customer, your spouse, a friend or to God, listening is critical to

the outcome of your conversation. Many people think that praying is only talking *to* God, when in reality, it is talking *with* God. There is an enormous difference.

Talking with God requires active listening. Stop and think about something for a moment. How do people communicate with you? Do they only use words? Do they only use their mouths? The truth is that they use words from their mouths and they send written messages like texts and emails. They use body language and tone of voice. They also communicate in other ways. There is a story about a wife who was so frustrated with her husband leaving the toilet seat up that he found it duct taped to the toilet bowl one day. His wife had not said a word, but he got the message loud and clear.

God also uses many different methods of communication. While rare, sometimes God uses an actual voice that we can hear. This is certainly not his primary method of communication, but the Bible does make it clear that God has used this method of communication in the past. God also speaks to us through messengers.

On several occasions, God sent an angel to deliver a message of critical importance. The Bible also tells us that sometimes the person receiving the message knows that they are communicating with an angel, but sometimes we do not. In other words, you may receive a message from someone you think is an ordinary person, but in actuality is an angel.

God's favorite method of communication is the Word that he gave us in the Bible. More often than not, the answer to our questions, requests and concerns lie within those sacred pages. Reality check; If you are not reading your Bible on a regular basis, you are not hearing most of what God is communicating to you. If you got a copy of this book that was randomly missing more than half of the words, do you think you would understand it?

Sometimes God speaks to us through other people, especially other believers. Over and over in the Bible, He tells us to seek the council of other Followers if we need wisdom or knowledge. The people you call Pastor, teacher, mentor, accountability partner or brother or sister in Christ can all be excellent conduits for God to communicate with you. One question I hear repeatedly is "How do I know that the advice or rebuke I received from someone is actually from God." There are two things you should always do to verify where the message is coming from. The first is the most important and many times the only step needed. Verify that the message the person gave you lines up with the Bible. If the message contradicts the Bible, it is not from God. If you are still not sure, you should pray. If you are skilled in listening to God, you may get your answer very quickly. If you are still not sure, you should seek the council of other believers. Be wise in who you ask advice from. Make sure the person you seek council from is a mature believer.

My personal favorite way that God communicates is that "Still, small voice" inside me. Sometimes you just know what to do, what to say (Or what not to say). This form of communication is one of the rarest for us to hear because we usually don't hear it. If you haven't practiced listening to God, it will be difficult to understand the message He is sending you. On the flip side, when you start to learn to listen, you will hear him more and more. It will bring you so much joy that you will crave to hear Him. It will inspire you to learn to listen better. It will also quickly make you aware of the loss of connection that comes from having un-repented sin in your life. When sin blocks your communication with God it will feel awful. You will crave to have it restored quickly, which through repentance we can easily do.

All of this leads back to quiet time. You must be intentional about creating a quiet time daily to hear from God.

If you set thirty minutes each day to pray, and then spend all thirty minutes talking to Him, you have allowed Him no time to answer you. Besides, who do you think might have more important things to talk about, you or God? Knowing that the Lord employs so many different methods of communication, you need to prepare yourself to listen. I would recommend that you have your Bible at your side when you are having your quiet time. You will likely find yourself directed to its pages as you learn to listen to God. Listening to God is a process, it will not happen overnight. You need to practice listening daily. The more you practice, the more you will hear Him. The more you hear Him, the more your faith will deepen, and as your faith grows and your communication with God increases, you will become more and more like Christ.

FELLOWSHIP

Brian was a close friend. We served together at our church and had many things in common. Both of us "Married up" and both of us had great kids. For those of you who are raising or have raised teenagers, you know how busy and demanding this season of life can be. It seemed like Brian and I were always running into each other at school functions. Many times we would sit together in the stands watching the Rockwall High School Yellow Jackets football team, marching band, drill team and cheerleaders as proud parents in our small Texas town. Brian and I were not just friends, we were doing life together.

As our kids got older, I started to notice some differences in Brian. As his life got busier and busier, he started to engage in fellowship with other believers less and less, forsaking church activities for school activities with his kids or golf with his buddies. Brian's priorities had him spending less time with other men who would encourage and strengthen him and more time with those who would distract him from his true purpose.

Brian was living his life in high gear. The more time he spent away from his Christian family, the weaker his relationship that mattered became. Soon his relationship with his kids became strained. Next his relationship with his wife became strained. Brian tried to compensate by spending more time with his wife and kids, but chose to cut out even more contact with other believers. Brian stepped down from his leadership position at the church. His life group attendance became erratic. Soon he wasn't even going to church on Sunday. Brian knew that going to church was important so he decided to try to get his family reengaged in a new church. Unfortunately, he chose a church that didn't do a lot of intentional fellowship, thinking that this might fit his family's busy lifestyle better.

Even though I reached out to Brian many times throughout this process, we eventually lost contact. For almost an entire year I heard not a peep from the man who was once one of my closest friends. Then, surprisingly, he showed up unannounced at a men's bible study one Saturday morning. I was excited to see my old friend and after the Bible study was over, I pulled him aside to have a private conversation.

"Are you coming back to church?" I asked. Brian said "Probably not, the wife and kids don't really want to go to church any more. I was just in the neighborhood and thought I would say hello." "Do you think that is okay?" I asked. Brian replied "No, but it is just my reality right now." "Brian, do you ever watch National Geographic?" I asked. Surprised, Brian says, "Well, sure." I continue, "Have you ever watched a lion attack a herd of animals?" "Yes." Brian said. I asked, "What does their strategy look like?" At this, Brian thought for a moment and then replied, "The lion will separate one animal from the herd and then attack and kill it." I said, "You are absolutely right Brian, and the Bible tells us that the Devil is like a prowling lion waiting for someone to devour. Brian, you are no longer in church. You are no longer spending time with other believers. Satan has you separated from the herd right now and if you don't get reconnected, he is going to destroy you. Brian, you know this is true. Please come back."

Brian chose not to return. Not long after our last meeting he was divorced and estranged from his kids and nearly thirty years of marriage and fathering had been destroyed. The Bible makes it very clear; we were designed to live in community with one another. The apostle Paul uses the analogy that we are all parts of a physical body. Each of us plays a unique part in the body of Christ, just as a nose is unique from a hand, so is the body better off with all of its parts acting together. The book of Acts is a beautiful illustration of fellowship. Acts details how believers are to go to church together, eat together, serve together and worship together. Fellowship is not just a privilege, it is a necessity if we are to thrive in the hostile environment of this fallen world.

WORSHIP

Worshiping God is any act that brings Glory to Him and, at the same time, reinforces the reality that God and his plan is perfect and holy while man in his natural state is weak and flawed, and his pursuits are petty and meaningless. This is why singing songs at church about the majesty of God (Regardless of if we are singing about the Father, Son or Holy Spirit) are called worship, but worship can be so much more.

Going on a mission trip, feeding the hungry in His name and witnessing about the changes in your life since you accepted Jesus as your Lord and Savior are all examples of worship. Giving your tithe is an act of worship as well, but how much greater is your sacrifice of your most precious resource – your time. The world tells us that you need to look out for number one; that you need to pursue those things that make you happy and bring fulfillment. The Bible tells us something very different. The Bible says we are to offer our bodies as a living sacrifice to God. That means we are supposed to realize that the things that matter to God are more important than the things that matter to us. We are to pursue the things that are important to God with all of our heart, mind and body. The amazing thing is that as we walk on this path, the things that matter to God start to matter to us. The closer we get to living the life that Jesus intended to live, we experience more joy, and most importantly, we begin to understand and experience significance.

One hot summer afternoon I was delivering food to a poor neighborhood not far from where I live. Our church partners would identify families in need and let me know where they lived. I would then let them know I would be by to deliver food. Being able to provide physical resources was great, but my true mission was to meet the families we were serving, understand their emotional and spiritual needs and pray with them, or if they did not know Christ, I would facilitate an introduction to Him. On this day, the neighborhood was unusually quiet. No one wanted to be in the heat that was radiating off the blacktop or the small brick houses that lined the street. It had rained recently and the humidity made it difficult to get a good breath of air into my lungs. The air was so moist, it felt like I was walking in the rain, although there was not a cloud in the sky.

I knocked on the door of a familiar house. I had been there several times before, but no adults were ever home. I assumed today would be no different, although I still carried the heavy box of food that included canned goods, shelf stable milk, dry pasta and other staples. The North Texas Food Bank had even had Wonder bread that week, so a loaf of bread with the familiar colored dots on the bag sat on top of the box I was carrying.

I was surprised when the door opened and there stood a 40-something year old Black lady dressed as if she were on her way to work. I introduced myself and she invited me into her home. Her name was Betty, and as I set her groceries on the kitchen counter, she told me that for some reason, she had decided to come home for lunch today, although she usually brought her lunch to work with her. Betty told me that had been the reason we had never met before, as she was normally working during the time I delivered food. Her two children were watching TV quietly in the living room. It was a cartoon that did not include Bugs Bunny, Wile E Coyote, Scooby Doo or any other familiar characters, reminding me of how different the world, and I, had become in just a few decades.

Betty explained that she had to return to work, and we walked onto the front porch. I asked her if she had anything that she would like me to pray for. She hesitated, but then gave me a prayer request having to do with her finances. I told Betty that I would like to pray for her now, while we were together, and as I spoke, the Holy Spirit was prompting me to ask another question. Before Betty could answer me, I asked "Betty, do you have a personal relationship with Christ?" Betty responded by saying "I grew up in church, so I have known about God since I was young." I paused. Her answer raised a red flag. She said she knew "About" Jesus, so I continued, "Betty, if something tragic happened today and you died, do you know where you would spend eternity?" Betty's face darkened a bit as if she were considering the question. She said "Well, I hope I would go to Heaven. I think I have been a good person."

What followed was a conversation about the redemptive power of grace and the free gift of salvation, culminating with the knowledge that once Betty made a decision to follow Jesus, she never had to worry about her eternal home again. Betty made a profession of faith right there on her porch and then went back into her house to tell share the good news with her children.

On that day, I had worshiped as a true believer. I gave my time and my attention to the things that mattered to God. I could have chosen to pursue other things that were important to me, but instead I brought glory to God with my obedience. The ironic thing is, I look back on that day as one of the most "Successful" days of my life. God used me that day to completely change to course of someone's life.

That day, God chose an ordinary man to do an extraordinary thing. God has a perfect plan for your life as well, and only through your continual acts of worship can you experience the significance that our Lord has prepared for you.

OTHERS SECOND

SERVICE

As he was nearing the end of his life, the Apostle Paul finds himself in prison again. Prisons in this day and age were nothing like the prisons we know today. Imagine being stripped and beaten with a leather strap until your chest and back were bloody and torn. If you had any ripped clothing left on your body it would not be replaced as you were shackled by the wrists or ankles into your cell. No medical treatment would be given and there were no bathroom facilities. Disease was rampant. The bitter cold of the stone walls and floor would make it nearly impossible to sleep and many of the other inmates would commit suicide before their sentences had been served to escape the nightmare they found themselves in.

Paul was no stranger to these surroundings. While in this particular prison he wrote a letter to the church in Philippi. This letter is one of the most encouraging communications that Paul ever wrote. In fact, if you ask many people what their favorite bible verse is, they will tell you that is one of the many famous passages from the book of Philippians. One of the most powerful themes in Philippians is finding contentment regardless of your circumstances. This theme is particularly relevant because Paul was writing to the church in Philippi from a prison and on a previous trip to Philippi, Paul had been thrown into a local prison and it was one of the harshest experiences of his life.

So here is a man, sitting in prison, writing to people who live in a place where Paul had one of the worst prison experiences of his life, and he writes some of the most encouraging, life giving passages in scripture. How can that be? The reason is clear. Paul put Jesus first, other people second and himself third. Paul found a way to be of service to others, even though he was locked up in a prison. He could not leave to preach or to physically serve others, so he found a way to have an impact and serve, even though his resources were few and his obstacles many.

How does your willingness to serve compare to Paul's? Most of us will fall woefully short of his example, but God gave us his example for a reason. Jesus came to serve, not to be served. Paul spent his life imitating what Jesus had done. We are to imitate Paul so that others can see us and follow in our footsteps. Service to others can take many forms and if you pray and ask God, it will become clear what service God has prepared for you to do. Many times, as I am discussing this topic with others, I hear things like "I am not sure what type of service I *want* to do." This attitude conflict with the whole "Others before self" concept and can rob us of the joy that God has prepared for us to experience through our service. Instead of asking what kind of service we want to do, we need to be asking what kind of service we were made to do. Once we figure out what God made us for and how he wired us, it is infinitely easier to hear and engage in service that will be most beneficial to others as well as ourselves.

Usually, our service and our spiritual gifts are connected. If you do not know what your spiritual gift or gifts are, then check out http://gifts.churchgrowth.org/analysis/index.php for more details on this subject.

GIVING

One day a wife was talking to her husband about investing for retirement while driving through their neighborhood. As they were discussing 401K's, IRA's and mutual funds, the husband noticed a house for sale just down the street from where they lived and asked his wife, "Do you think God will ever bless us with the resources to buy a rental house?" His wife thought for a moment and then asked her husband a question, "If God did give us the resources to buy a rental house, and then later asked us to give it away to someone for free, do you think you would be able to do that?" Now it was the husband who was deep in thought. After several moments he replied, "Probably not. I would like to say yes, but probably not." His wife then replied "Then that is my answer to whether God will bless us with the resources to buy a rental house. Probably not. He would like to say yes, but probably not."

How is your heart for giving? Do you hold tightly to the resources God has given you? God commands us to give ten percent because He knows it will sting just enough to get our attention. The funny thing is that most of us don't even give the minimum required, and the ten percent was designed to just be a warm up. If you want to be a steward of many resources then you have to give wisely regarding the ones you already have.

If you are not already tithing, start increasing your giving and ramp up to ten percent as soon as you possibly can. I need to be clear on this, tithing is your giving directly to your local church. It does not include giving to other causes, or paying for a mission trip or giving money to your friend who is in need. You should give to those things, but they are not included in your tithe. They are on top of your tithe. Give at least ten percent to your local church first, then feel free to give gifts and offerings above that amount as God leads you.

If you have not already experienced the power of giving, then buckle up. God gives resources to those who are faithful, so if you want to steward more, you need to give more.

You will be successful if you follow this formula: Jesus first and others second. The world's economy runs on a "Self" first philosophy, and many millions of people live lonely, empty lives in pursuit of a plan that is destined to fail. Don't fall into that trap. God's economy runs differently and it leads to a life of abundance and joy.

CHAPTER 15

WHAT NOW?

CONNECT TO GOD – Do you know Jesus as your Lord and Savior? If you do, then you are blessed.

Do you know Jesus, but feel disconnected right now? I love the word picture of Jesus walking behind us wherever we go. We can run, but we can't out run Jesus. We can hide, but we can't hide from Jesus. No matter where we go, regardless of how far off the path God laid out for us, Jesus is right behind us. He pursues us the way a father pursues his child who has walked off into the wilderness. He pursues us, calling our name, desperate to get our attention to lead us away from danger. That father, Jesus, is right behind you. Simply turn around and He is there, ready and desperate to show you His love. All you need to do is turn around.

Are you still thinking about God? If so, please read the last chapter, I wrote it specifically for you.

Connect to Church – Many of you have had bad experiences with your local church. I once heard someone say "Church would be great if it were not for the Christians there." People are not perfect. In fact, some of them are downright broken and can act in terrible ways. While all of that is true, God created His church for a reason; the assembling of His followers for training and worship. God warns us about the potential consequences of failing to gather in church and they usually end with being devoured by a lion. If you don't currently have a church home, go and find one. Visit as many as you need to, but keep looking. God has a church home for you, and he intends for it to be a blessing. On a side note; if you have been to a dozen churches and none of them seem to be a fit, the problem is likely not with the churches, it is with you. Pray. Seek His will and be courageous enough to engage with other believers in corporate worship.

Connect to Small Group - A small group, usually twenty to fifty people, is imperative to your spiritual growth. If you current church does not have small groups, then consider starting one yourself. Acts 2 tells us that the very first church had small groups of people gathering together for study, fellowship and accountability. Before you label me as a "Small church guy" also remember that the very first church saw 3000 people come to Christ on its very first day, making it a mega-church. God also knew that we would not thrive in an environment that large, so He created a system of small groups within the church to tend to the needs of the people. This is the Church within the Church that makes discipleship possible.

Continue Training – In this book you have learned The Base, The Blocks and The Blueprint to build a successful sales career. Have you committed them to memory? Are they part of your sales toolkit? If not, then you must do the following:

Continue Practicing – Practice is the key to making these skills part of your sales toolkit. The more you practice, the more they will become muscle memory, and the better you will become. As I am writing this book, the Olympics are underway in Rio. I heard the story of a gymnast who started her training at three years old. They say she spends over 30 hours a week perfecting her craft and even more over the last four years as the Olympics approached. Are you that serious about your career? Are you that committed? Most of us spend more than thirty hours per week doing our jobs, so imagine what we can accomplish if you really focus on improvement on every sales call, every day. The Apostle Paul said He was in a race and in pursuit of victory. Are you?

CHAPTER 16
THE MOST IMPORTANT
CHAPTER OF ALL

WHO IS JESUS?

SIMPLY PUT, JESUS is the perfect sacrifice for the sins that you and I have committed. Before God sent His Son to Earth, he gave us a list of attributes that were very unique so we could be sure we were really following the Son of God and not an imposter. We call this prophecy. One of the attributes would be that the Son of God would be born of a virgin mother. This one alone would greatly narrow the field, so to speak, but God gave us many qualifications to know His Son. I am not going to get into all of them here, but I would suggest you check them out for yourself.

When God created the Earth, he created it without sin, but we (starting with Adam and Eve) messed that up. God cannot exist in the presence of sin, so the punishment for sin is the eternal separation from God. Before God sent His Son, people would repent (agree with God that what they did was wrong and turn away from that behavior) of their sins and offer a sacrifice to God. Animals were precious to early society, and a sin offering to God had to be the best of your flock, so it hurt, encouraging you not to do that behavior again. When God sent His Son, He sent us the perfect sin offering because Jesus lived his entire life without ever committing a sin. Imagine you have been convicted of a crime and stand before the judge to receive your sentence. The judge tells you what your punishment is and then someone else steps up and says "I will take the punishment in his place." That is what Jesus did and does for us. He was able to do this because while He was with us he was fully God and fully man at the same time. No one but God could ever have done this and because he was also fully man, Jesus had the ability to sin and yet chose not to. He is the only perfect man to have ever lived, so God accepts his death in place of yours.

Here is the Gospel in a nut shell. Jesus, the Son of God, was born from a virgin mother, lived a perfect life free of sin and was crucified on a cross as a perfect sacrifice for the sins that you and I have committed. He died on that cross, was buried, and then on the third day, Jesus rose from the dead. He appeared to hundreds of people so that we would know that He had truly defeated death, which gives us confidence that we will experience the same resurrection after our physical deaths. Jesus then ascended to Heaven, where he acts as the intermediator for us to God.

Here is the really Good News. The only thing we have to do for Jesus to step in and take our punishment is believe that He is the Son of God; who he claimed to be. If we believe with our hearts, and say with our mouths that Jesus is the one and only Son of God then we will be saved. When you receive this gift, you will be compelled to live a life for Christ, making Him Lord of your life.

WHY ARE WE HERE?

Often times I hear about new Christians who are excited about the forgiveness they have received but don't really know what is next. Accepting Christ as your Savior is different from accepting Him as Lord. Being born again is not the end of the journey, it is the beginning. The Gospel of Matthew clearly lays out our mission on Earth. The job of a believer is to take the Good News of Jesus and share it with their home and local community, neighboring areas that are different from our own and even to the farthest reaches of our planet. This does not mean that every person is called to be a vocational missionary, but it does mean that we are called to live our lives on mission for Jesus. Being a follower of Jesus means we put His agenda first, and His plan for our lives is far greater and far more enriching than our own plans could ever be.

HOW DO I ACCEPT CHRIST?

Are you ready to live your new life? Are you ready to experience freedom from guilt and understand what joy is for the first time? If you are, then pray this prayer:

Jesus, I believe that you are God's one and only Son. I believe that you defeated death and that you died on that cross for me, because you love me. I am a sinner, and I don't deserve the gift that you are giving me, but I accept your forgiveness. I trust you to be my savior and I commit to make you my Lord. Please accept my life as an offering to you, for all that you have done for me and help me to be faithful. Thank you for saving me. Amen.

Welcome to the family of God. I am now your brother and you are my brother or sister. Your first step as a new believer is to be baptized. Baptism is simply a public profession of your faith. It is not necessary for salvation, but it is your first step of obedience in letting Christ be Lord of your life. The Bible tells us that every time a person accepts Christ, the angels throw a party in Heaven. They are high fiving each other right now because of what you have just done. Welcome to your new family and welcome to your new life.

ACKNOWLEDGEMENTS

I WANT TO thank my Proverbs 31 wife Dena and my three inspiring kids, Allison, John Jr., and Lauren for all or their support, encouragement, advice and editing help.

I also want to thank Dr. Ben Voth, Sean Wilson, Jeff Gouldie and Randy Eilts for their dedication to the Word and accuracy.

Special thanks to Paul Pop and Lyle Caddell for holding me accountable when I needed it most.

Thanks to the Kimmel Life Group for encouraging me to walk on God's path and to all my friends who pushed and carried me along the way.

To my mother who spent countless hours on her knees praying for my soul and my father who was my first sales trainer.

To Kary Oberbrunner I want to say thank you for lighting the author fire that was smoldering inside of me. If we had not met, I'm not sure the flames would ever have ignited.

To Pastor Steve Stroope who took time out of his incredibly busy schedule to read and subsequently endorse my book. I am honored.

Finally, thank you to Pastor John Stone. My life in Christ was changed forever because of the light and salt you provided in my life, and I am eternally grateful.

ABOUT THE AUTHOR

JOHN J. KIMMEL is a professional salesperson who started his sales career in the floor covering business in 1984. He advanced into sales management in 1988 and has spent over 30 years developing his sales skills, managing salespeople and training sales professionals. His experience includes wholesale and retail on a local, regional and national level.

John's wife introduced him to Christ in 1992. Since then, he has served as a teacher to men, couples and singles. John's passion is training leadership, especially in countries and places where resources are limited and governments stand opposed to Christianity. Kimmel is a certified John C. Maxwell leadership trainer and has trained on leadership, the Bible and sales on a constant basis for over two decades.

Selling with power is the result of John's vocational and spiritual worlds colliding to solve one simple problem; how do you sell with power and effectiveness in such a way that will change your life and the lives of your family while being in a constant state of the will of God.

END NOTES

Chapter 1:   James 2:14-26; 2 Corinthians 5:11;
Romans 4:20-21; Acts 28:23; Mark 9:30-37;
John 13:34-35; Luke 16:10; Colossians 3:23;
Jeremiah 29:11

Chapter 2:   Philippians 2:3-4

Chapter 4:   James 2:8

Chapter 5:   Proverbs 12:27;

Chapter 6:   Proverbs 13:4 (NIV); Proverbs 13:4 (NLT);
Romans 12:10

Chapter 10: Matthew 12:11; Matthew 6:27;
Matthew 9:28; How Many Seconds to a First
Impression? By Eric Wargo.1 seconds to a
first impression; *Deprez-Sims, Anne-Sophie;
Morris, Scott B. "Accents in the workplace: Their
effects during a job interview".International Journal
of Psychology* **45** *(6): 417–426.*

Chapter 12: Proverbs 6:6-8

Chapter 13: Romans 12:3; James 1:17;
2 Corinthians 5:17; Colossians 2:10;
1 Peter 1:23; Romans 8:37; Ephesians 1:7;
1 Peter 2:9; Romans 8:2; Ephesians 2:10;
Ephesians 2:5; Isaiah 54:14; 1 John 5:18;
Ephesians 1:4; 1 Peter 1:16;
1 Corinthians 2:16; Philippians 4:7;
Romans 5:17; Ephesians 4:17-18;
Mark 4:17-18; Philippians 4:19;
Philippians 4:13; Romans 8:17;
Revelation 12:11; 2 Peter 1:3-4;
2 Corinthians 5:20; 1 Peter 2:9;
1 Corinthians 6:19; Romans 8:33;
Galatians 3:13; Colossians 1:13;
2 Timothy 1:9; Colossians 1:11;
Romans 1:7; http://www.joycemeyer.org/
articles/ea.aspx?article=knowing_who_i_
am_in_christ; https://bible.org/seriespage/
lesson-35-take-care-how-you-listen-luke-816-21

Chapter 14: 2 Timothy 2:15; 1 Corinthians 12:12-31;
Matthew 20:28

56538597R00088

Made in the USA
Columbia, SC
27 April 2019